Dieter Adler

What We Truly Need
Experiences of a Psychoanalyst

Dieter Adler

WHAT WE TRULY NEED

Experiences of a Psychoanalyst

Bibliografische Information der Deutschen Nationalbibliothek
Die Deutsche Nationalbibliothek verzeichnet diese Publikation in der Deutschen Nationalbibliografie; detaillierte bibliografische Daten sind im Internet über http://dnb.d-nb.de abrufbar.

Bibliographic information published by the Deutsche Nationalbibliothek
The Deutsche Nationalbibliothek lists this publication in the Deutsche Nationalbibliografie; detailed bibliographic data are available on the Internet at http://dnb.d-nb.de.

© 2022 (original German edition) Dieter Adler: *Was wir wirklich brauchen. Erfahrungen eines Psychoanalytikers.* Verlag: Schattauer

Editing: Gabriele Wever, Karla Seedorf (original German manuscript), Kerstin Lange, Nancy Chapple (English translation)

Cover picture: ID 108122215 © Evgenyatamanenko | Dreamstime.com

ISBN (Print): 978-3-8382-1946-2
ISBN (E-Book [PDF]): 978-3-8382-7946-6
© *ibidem*-Verlag, Hannover • Stuttgart 2025

Alle Rechte vorbehalten

Leuschnerstraße 40
30457 Hannover
Germany / Deutschland
info@ibidem.eu

Das Werk einschließlich aller seiner Teile ist urheberrechtlich geschützt. Jede Verwertung außerhalb der engen Grenzen des Urheberrechtsgesetzes ist ohne Zustimmung des Verlages unzulässig und strafbar. Dies gilt insbesondere für Vervielfältigungen, Übersetzungen, Mikroverfilmungen und elektronische Speicherformen sowie Einspeicherung und Verarbeitung in elektronischen Systemen.

All rights reserved. No part of this publication may be reproduced, stored in or introduced into a retrieval system, or transmitted, in any form, or by any means (electronic, mechanical, photocopying, recording or otherwise) without the prior written permission of the publisher. Any person who commits any unauthorized act in relation to this publication may be liable to criminal prosecution and civil claims for damages.

Printed in the EU

*For my wife Marion,
and my children Eike, Leah Emily, and Fiete*

Content

Foreword 9

1. Introduction 15
   1.1 Preliminary remarks 16
   1.2 Acknowledgements 20
   1.3 What is important? 21
   1.4 What does it take to be satisfied? 24

2. In community and with each other 25
   2.1 Community and the feeling of security 26
   2.2 Companions 29
   2.3 Security 31
   2.4 Mirroring and support 32
   2.5 Dealing with others 35

3. Feelings 39
   3.1 Affection 40
   3.2 Loneliness and devotion 43
   3.3 Closeness 45
   3.4 Thoughts versus feelings 54
   3.5 Sensuality 63
   3.6 Pleasure 71
   3.7 Curiosity 77

4. Active engagement 79
   4.1 Postponement 80
   4.2 Career choice 86
   4.3 Success 97
   4.4 Self-efficacy 103
   4.5 Heart and passion 106

	4.6 Chaos	110
	4.7 Time and money	112
5.	**Responsibility and self-care**	**115**
	5.1 Authentic	116
	5.2 Courage	121
	5.3 Caring and self-care	123
	5.4 Security in oneself	129
	5.5 Six thousand euros are enough	132
	5.6 Win-win situations	134
6.	**Self-sabotage**	**139**
	6.1 Possession	140
	6.2 Playing a Role	142
	6.3 Superiority	147
	6.4 Disrespect	149
	6.5 Carelessness	152
7.	**Becoming human**	**157**
	7.1 Respect for the weak	158
	7.2 Time and patience	160
	7.3 Slowness	162
	7.4 First things first	164
	7.5 Modesty and humility	167
	7.6 The meaning of life	169
	7.7 What is happiness?	173
Literature		**177**
About the author		**179**
	More books by Dieter Adler:	181

Foreword

Psychotherapy:
Essence, Experience, and Examination

In any serious, scientific, and ethically justified healthcare profession, the focus should be always on the overall health, treatment, improvement, and amelioration of the patient. What clinical and professional background should therefore a mental health professional have?

Dieter Adler might appear as a true Renaissance man, even a polymath. In fact, he is not only a psychotherapist, psychoanalyst, group analyst, and child and youth therapist, but also a supervisor, a teacher, a filmmaker, as well as the founder and chair of the German Network of Psychotherapists. While one ought to refrain from any "argument from authority, prestige, fame, or title" in deciding which therapeutic method to utilize, one also has to admit that the aforementioned background makes for a very solid case. So, what is, then, that we "truly need?"

In his book, Adler does not want to simply offer a quick guide to self-help. In fact, he is clear about the fact that this is not the purpose of the book: "Maybe I'll write one sometime: *How you can reliably become independent of self-help books.*" In fact, this book is a reflection on a 30-year-long professional career in which the author has learned to ask questions, to listen attentively, and to help shed light on some of the most complex and hidden aspects of what makes us human. To be sure, this does not mean that this book does not present a practical approach to well-being — quite the contrary. The author lists a series of areas the patient can focus on, in order to achieve a higher state of balance, healing, and happiness. Amongst these we find socialization, upbringing, and community, making friends, understanding and working on one's emotions and the emotions of others, staying physically and mentally active, finding a sense of security and confidence, maintaining a sense of curiosity, finding a work-life balance and rediscovering peace and calmness, having goals, purposes, and meaning in life, and of course, understanding those negative, self-sabotaging mechanisms and processes which hinder such developments.

In this sense, Adler might remind us of other scholars and researchers such as Abraham Maslow, but his work is, by his own admission, closer to that of Igor Caruso and Arno Gruen. In fact, in the last part of this volume, one could find influences as wide and far as Viktor Emil von Gebsattel or Rudolf Allers. This also means that Adler's work is important not only from a clinical perspective, but also from a social one. In his attentive and insightful analysis, Adler juxtaposes very difficult and profound concepts such as Chaos and Passion to very practical areas of self-improvement, for instance motivation and job search. Furthermore, the author's ethics are apparent throughout the book, which is essential in any advice on how to help fellow human beings. In Chapter 5, *Responsibility and self-care*, Dieter Adler writes that "This chapter is particularly close to my heart." And it shows in the particular care he displays in analyzing it.

What is even more interesting, and useful to the person who is looking for guidance, motivation, and help, is the fact that Adler does not shy away from stating the difficulties of such a process, in a clear and direct manner. He writes: "We humans always live in a contradiction between needs that benefit ourselves and needs that benefit the community." The author's approach is nurturing and kind, yet firm and balanced.

Dieter Adler also embraces one of the most useful pieces of advice in psychotherapy, namely the fact that thoughts and emotions are not the same. More in detail, thoughts and emotions do not always align, which means that they might be disconnected, or that they might need to be kept at a healthy distance, in order to master self-care and self-control. The same can be said about action. In other words, one needs to be very careful to avoid being led only by strong emotions in life. One also needs to understand that "thoughts are just thoughts" sometimes, and that we are not forced to act upon them. In Chapter 3, Adler writes that: "Thoughts are an attempt to interrupt the immediacy of reactions that follow feelings and to deconstruct and reconstruct the triggering situation without feeling or affect, and above all without fear. Instead of running away from the fire, it may make sense to head straight for it and risk burns rather than being suffocated by the smoke in a dead end." This helps face our inner demons, label them and put them in their proper place. This is also key to progressive exposure and response prevention, a fundamental psychotherapeutic technique in dealing with traumas and obsessive-compulsive disorder. And Adler knows this very well.

Elsewhere in the book, Adler talks about "deconstructing and reconstructing." Certainly, one could see how this might be much more aligned with a sense of "suspension of judgment" in the neo-post-modernist, neo-psychoanalytic tradition. It is nevertheless interesting to observe that the very last two sections of the book deal with "The Meaning of Life" and "What is Luck?" These are certainly not lines of investigation traditionally (pun intended) aligned with the contemporary versions of deconstructivism or hyper-relativism, which are less interested in discovering and discussing truth and reality than in a puritanistic moralizing stance against anything these two terms represent.

And yet, the author does not offer here any shortcuts or even the slightest guidance in a universalist sense. He writes that "The meaning of life is as meaningless as the philosopher's stone." In this sense, i.e. the "sense of the ultimate lack of sense," the author appears to follow the most common postmodernist tropes fighting against anything certain, anything universal, anything truly valuable, from true statements to moral rules, to mathematics and logic. And yet, the author is also ready to acknowledge that the reason—the "true meaning" one could infer or, perhaps, deduce—for this attitude is to save patients, hurt individuals who are internally and externally broken, suffering, and struggling, from becoming preys of self-styled and impromptu-improvised gurus, who might offer false promises in exchange for further pain and enduring desperation.

Certainly, one could still argue with the stance against objective or universal meaning in life, but one has to acknowledge the importance and the ethics of *primum non nocere* ("First, do no harm") in protecting patients from hurt, damage, and abusive relationships of all kinds. In this sense, we can then understand the essence, experience, and examination of psychotherapy. It is, after all, a rediscovery of truth and reality, which not only protects individuals from self harm and being harmed by others, but also sheds light on the path toward self-discovery, against fallacies, ideologies, and brainwashing. *What we Truly Need, indeed.* Said by a true psychotherapist.

Acad. Prof. Dr. David Tomasi

1. Introduction

1.1 Preliminary remarks

What We Truly Need may at first sound somewhat "biblical" or prophetic. Here, I'll have to disappoint the reader. It's merely a collection of insights after thirty years on the other side of the couch. When people have come to me for counseling or treatment, they were invariably suffering from the seemingly simple things: a loss of courage, no purpose in life, loneliness, a sense of meaninglessness, and so on. I never saw anyone who suffered from their unemployment or the loss of their partner. This was certainly the "entry point" for seeking help, but, after a short time, it turned out that quite different inner adversities were making life difficult for the person who had come to see me.

Existential questions are often disconnected from the external things of our outward lives. External things, more often than not, embody an illusory security; the insecure or inhibited person clings to them so as not to lose his or her grip. As a rule, however, they are of as little use as a tennis racket in a lifeboat.

At the end of the treatment, it was the "seemingly simple" things, the seemingly easily achievable goals or circumstances, that counted—like friendship, a sense of security, confidence, having found a goal in life, having rediscovered curiosity, taking everything more calmly. But above all: being able to live from within again, instead of being an automaton at the mercy of external or internal forces. In short, being able to live more authentically. What mattered was to no longer do what one was not willing to do, but to engage in those things that truly bring satisfaction. I'm very grateful to my patients for these insights. I wrote this book on their behalf—it would not have been possible without their invaluable experiences.

Learning to be human is not easy, even in psychotherapy. First, we have to become more human ourselves. After much training, my supervision under Irvin Yalom, a very human but also very strict American psychoanalyst, helped me enormously and shaped my path. My relationships with my colleagues and friends Margarethe Mitscherlich and Sudhir Kakar were also formative. I'm also indebted to my spiritual and intellectual mentors Igor Caruso and Arno Gruen, whose mental attitudes I've adopted in fundamental respects.

I'm grateful to all of them.

This book rotates through gendered pronouns, but when I write in any gender, I mean all genders—all those known so far and all those yet to be discovered. I always speak of human beings.

After long discussions with myself and others, I've come to refrain from giving explicit advice. I think the whole book can inspire self-reflection, if that is what you want. If in the end it is only good to light a fire in the fireplace, then so be it, though I would prefer constructive criticism.

I find that the ability to reflect, which is important for our own development, has been on the decline far too much due to increasing convenience—or laziness. People get "their opinion" from the internet or from self-help books that tell you what you should do, change, or cease doing. Maybe I'll write one sometime: *How You Can Reliably Become Independent of Self-Help Books*.

My best experiences in therapy haven't been when I convinced someone of something or pushed the person to do something. Instead, they have been when I was able to stimulate a thought process that led first to a realization, then to an inner confrontation, then to a changed attitude, and finally to a change in the patient's behavior. In this way, it became part of his or her own person, rather than a following of my (supposed) beliefs. In therapy, not only is it important to ask the right questions, but the questions also have to fit the patient — as well as his current context. If a patient is dissatisfied with his partnership, asking him about success in his job will not accomplish much. Instead, I could ask this patient, if it feels appropriate, "Why do each of your partnerships fail when a woman commits to you?" The patient can then reflect on that and ask himself whether it's true. And if it is, the question of why arises automatically. Along with it, questions about one's own attitude may also arise. Am I just afraid of closeness and commitment, or do I not want a firm commitment at all, but rather variety? Or both?

These considerations are then not mine but his own: his personal attitudes, desires, and the conflicts that result from them. At some point he is in a deconstructivist process, at the end of which, as in every deconstructivist process, stands (indivisible) reality. I deliberately do not say truth, because reality and truth often diverge (it is, for example, true = that humans are polygamous by nature, but many partners do not want to pursue this or to allow the other to do so = reality).

In a nutshell: The patient must come to terms with his or her own realities.

One patient was looking for a partner who was educated, rich, intelligent, athletic as well as successful, had a certain social status, and was under twenty-six years old. He had to find out this was virtually impossible. And if it were possible, there would be very few specimens.

Once he realized this, I asked him to put himself in the role of such a potential partner and to ask himself what standards this woman, in turn, might have for a partner.

This was a new reality for him, one he had previously blocked out. Anyone so successful and attractive also, logically, has standards. In such situations, I like to add a question: "Tell me, while we're at it: What do you actually have to offer a woman like that?"
Well, that's how I work.

This book is—and is intended as—an invitation to reflect. And to smile now and then.

La Gomera, Canary Islands, August 2022

1.2 Acknowledgements

I would like to thank everyone who helped me with this book.

My thanks go to Marion Langer for her patient reading, constructive criticism, and valuable input. I would like to thank Karla Seedorf for the final editing, in which I found her to be very collaborative.

Thanks also to Dr. Nadja Urbani from Klett-Cotta Verlag for her openness and patience. I would especially like to thank Gabriele Wever for her sharp mind and the clarity with which she supported me in writing the book through patient co-shaping, correcting, and consistent proofreading. Without her, I doubt the project would have come this far.

1.3 What is important?

In many years of psychotherapy, I have often asked myself what really matters in life.

The question we must ask ourselves is: What is truly important in our lives? What makes us happy? What do we really need? On closer examination of this question, we will probably come to the realization that we don't need much to be happy. And we may see that it's not the things we expect, such as money, success in life, or material security. No, it's the simple things that make us content and that we need. They are human things, all too human things. The reflections I would like to share with readers come from many psychotherapeutic conversations with unhappy or at least dissatisfied people. Even if the roadblocks to a contented life are often due to patients' own self-impediments, this was usually not the sole cause of their suffering. Even when it was possible to remove the blockages, the majority of my patients were still unhappy. Apparently, it was not enough to break down the walls of their prisons. On the contrary, many did not want to emerge from their prisons at all. Now, one might jump to the conclusion that the reason was fear of life outside prison. My late colleague Arno Gruen, whom I was privileged to get to know in the last year of his life, stated that, in his experience, many people cannot live a free life, either because they do not want to take on the responsibility or because they are afraid of the disobedience necessary for a free life. This may apply for many of my patients, yet, in my experience, it's not enough to explain the persistence of their unhappiness.

I believe it's important and necessary to turn patients into rebels: rebels who rebel against conditions hostile to life and the people who create or maintain these conditions. Although in psychotherapy we can usually find out quickly against whom and what we should and must rebel, patients often lack the strength for rebellion. This was an enigma to me for some time, one which could not be solved even upon consulting with savvy supervisors. Until, one day, the scales fell from my eyes: The patients had nothing to fight for. They had many things they could and should fight against, but freedom would have brought them a condition that might be worse: inner emptiness. A patient once described it like this: "I no longer suffer from depression, but now what? What do I have left now?"

Another described the process of his psychoanalysis like cleaning out a flat, where even the secret dirty corners were not spared. In the end, after getting rid of all the ballast and everything unusable, he had the feeling of standing in an empty flat. On top of this, and above all, he was standing there alone, because in therapy he had also gotten rid of his unsatisfactory friendships.

For me, this vicariously solved the puzzle on behalf of all the other patients who felt the same or similar. I concluded that an intermediate step was necessary. For myself, the idea of an empty flat and a streamlined portfolio of friendships was a tantalizing one. After all, I could redesign everything and choose the furniture I had been wanting for a long time, and in the future spend my time only with people I really wanted to spend it with. The idea of a new beginning held something advantageous for me, something that gave me energy. But it made my patients more afraid, and that robbed them of their energy.

That's when I realized they had no idea what they needed and what was good for them. You can't go to a furniture store and choose new furnishings if you don't know what you want. The same applies to people or activities. Many patients give up activities during therapy that seemed natural before but may no longer mean anything to them. Often this happens without a conscious decision. They lose sight of friends and activities inadvertently. Only much later do they notice bonds have petered out that were once meaningful to them. It's like accidentally leaving behind an unimportant item and later making no effort to get it back.

Observing this led me to conclude that many people do not know what they really need, what does them good. I decided to investigate this phenomenon more closely.

1.4 What does it take to be satisfied?

"You don't need much to be happy. It just has to be the right thing," my training analyst once said to me. And I think it's true. At least, that has been and continues to be my experience. Not only in my own life, but also from my experience with many patients. But I have to disagree with him on one thing: Happiness is a highly potent drug, one which, like any drug, can cause addiction and dependency. The price for the absence of the happiness drug is unhappiness. In my own developmental process, I have replaced the term happiness with contentment. This is much more relaxed. For me, happiness is when I submit my tax return late, but the computers in the tax office crash at that very same moment.

So, what is it, then, that makes us content? The first thing we need is other people. We like to delude ourselves that we're able to get along without other people, or with only limited contact with others, or even that it's better to do so. It's true that others can become a burden or even impede us in our development. Many people have only perverted relationships where they maintain contact merely because they hope to gain something from it. Some people cannot build relationships with others because they are afraid of rejection or being taken advantage of. But even though this may sound banal and self-evident to many, the problem is: We need relationships that are satisfying for both sides. In my many years of psychotherapy, I have yet to meet a person whose suffering was not related to at least one unsatisfying relationship.

2. In community and with each other

2.1 Community and the feeling of security

When people come to me, I don't see them as sick people but as people seeking help, people who are stuck at a point in their lives and can't get out of the tight spot on their own. What I have noticed in thirty years is that all patients had two areas of conflict and suffered in either one or, not uncommonly, both. Many came to me with relationship difficulties. I basically mean all this person's interpersonal ties, but most often their primary partnership was concerned.

The other area of conflict was one's profession. A wrongly chosen partner can mar your life just as much as a wrongly chosen profession or job can. I'll discuss the choice of profession later. Let's start with why interpersonal relationships are so essential.

Satisfying relationships don't only stabilize our psyche and our self, but they also shape them in the first place. Unsatisfying relationships can deform them, that's also true. Fortunately, our life begins with two other people who, at best, are well-disposed toward us, who perceive us, react to our utterances, and enter into the mutual contact with us that we call communication. Closeness results. Interpersonal closeness is our most important need, and for the sake of its benefit, in the best scenario—namely if the relationship is satisfying—we give up our self-centered and selfish motives. But especially now, many people are afraid of this closeness. I will discuss the reasons for this later.

The feeling of closeness, when it can be lived without fear, is in itself a great source of joy and satisfaction.

When people additionally have the good fortune to live in a stable community and thus with many satisfying relationships, the basic need for security and protection is also satisfied. Precisely, these communities are experienced as very satisfying and free of fear. They foster courage, confidence, and trust in the world and in oneself. Unfortunately, in our culture these communities are exceedingly rare. I have mostly found them in my engagement with other cultures. Among the Zanskari, a people living in the Indian state of Kashmir in the second Himalayan range in villages where there is no electricity or water supply, I felt part of their community after a short time. A serious illness, a complicated fracture, would probably have meant certain death. Nevertheless, I felt safe and secure in a way I had never consciously experienced before. I emphasize "consciously" here, because I believe I knew this feeling as a small child, during a time of which I have no memory. The feeling of happiness matched the feeling of being in love. Our upbringing is an adaptation of our abilities to the demands of reality, and it causes us to lose this feeling of fundamental parental protection. Perhaps we don't lose it completely, but, after perceiving the "outside," we can no longer nestle into it as comfortably and naively. This is no different in communal cultures, but the security of the community remains with their members for life. Among the Ovahimba in Namibia, the individual maternal bond is quickly complemented by a bond with all the women of the village. All women become the child's mother, which led a colleague to coin the term "village mother."

In our culture, we are losing the feeling of security. This is partly because healthy communities are few and far between and partly because new communities cannot easily be constructed artificially. If the conditions from our early sense of security are not present, the whole thing fails. It's no different in psychotherapy: If the patient does not feel secure, the therapy is doomed to fail.

Because we can't live without a feeling of security, and we no longer get that feeling in communities, we seek and find it in our love relationships. The fact that love relationships have become a substitute for community ties in the Western world engenders new problems for many: the constant fear of losing a relationship, but also the perpetual discrepancy between our attachment needs and our inherent human needs for freedom and vagabondism. Neither of these problems occur in communal cultures, where temporary vagabondism is tolerated, and the fear of the loss of attachment is not a constant presence. Because people have a bond with the community, they can allow themselves to disagree or have a row with an individual. Being thrown out of a village community is the ultimate punishment in such communal cultures. Incidentally, this also protects the community and the individual from proscribed actions, which we would call criminal offenses.

2.2 Companions

In western cultures, as in communal cultures, all people have a need for companions. Mastering life alone is difficult and unsatisfying. Life with a like-minded person by my side is easier and more satisfying than alone. And experience shows that people with supporters are more successful. A good bond is not enough here; the companion must also identify with the other person's goals. This task is performed first by parents, then by friends or siblings. In our culture, partners often replace friends and siblings as companions. In communal cultures, friends and siblings remain companions. This is partly because our siblings or friends usually take different paths than we do. Rarely do we live in the same place after our individuation. This is different in communal cultures. Here, one traditionally stays in the community, spending one's whole life with them. The individual always has access to the people in his or her age group. In my experience, there is something else essential in communal cultures: Others are drawn on as only transient or temporary companions. Here, with an unconscious intelligence, a person seeks out a helpful supporter who can identify with the goal one wants to achieve or who is currently going through the same development.

When we no longer have communities, we fall back on love partners in this regard as well. This often leads to difficulties because the other person does not always have the same goals, may even be opposed to a goal, and also does not always have the same developmental tasks to contend with, or prefers perhaps to cope with them alone or to seek support from someone else, for example, someone of the same gender.

In addition, a phenomenon may then occur in love relationships that I have called "making someone into a sibling" or a "Hansel and Gretel marriage": one's partner not only loses his role as a sexually desirable person but can even end up in an aversive position in which sexuality becomes a taboo. This phenomenon has also been described by Westermarck (1902) and Shepher (1983).

2.3 Security

We don't like to be lonely. Humans are social creatures. When traveling alone, we don't like to take a seat in empty restaurants or cafés. Even if we don't know the other guests, they give us a bit of a feeling of security and safety — that's one of the reasons why literary cafés experienced a heyday in Vienna and Paris in the last century. Security is a basic need we cannot achieve without others. Sometimes, of course, particular spaces can create a sense of security even without other people. However, I believe that, in such cases, memories involving experiences of security with other people are mobilized from the unconscious. We see a room that has elements of our grandmother's living room, where we always felt very much at home and safe. We may not remember the details of grandmother's living room. Rather, we unconsciously remember the feeling of security, triggered by an old sofa or the smell of a room where we feel safe in the here and now. A patient once confessed to me that he had designed his living room at home exactly like my consulting room. Despite many erotic adventures, he was a profoundly lonely person who dared to admit for the first time during treatment — especially to himself — that he lacked a feeling of security and was very afraid of engaging with it. I will talk about this fear later.

2.4 Mirroring and support

It's thanks to the psychoanalyst Heinz Kohut that we now have a precise idea of how our self-esteem develops and what we need to keep it stable. Only a few elements are necessary to help a young person develop a stable and healthy sense of self-esteem. First, the "gleam in the mother's eye" is important so that the infant feels not only seen (i.e., perceived as existing) but also feels that others take pleasure in his existence. We retain this existential need throughout our lifetime. When we join a new group, accept a new job, or get to know someone, it feels good to see the gleam in others' eyes. We notice and feel that the other person or people take pleasure in us. And what a bad start it is when we're only greeted matter-of-factly or, even more calamitously, are received warily or suspiciously.

At the same time, the gleam in the eyes of the other person must be honest, must "come from within." Authenticity in the encounter is another essential human need and a basic prerequisite for satisfying human contacts and relationships. Any form of feigned, artificial, acquired, or forced friendliness impedes direct contact and closeness to the other. We can easily recognize when another person is being dishonest, even though feigned friendliness or feigned interest seems to have become the norm in our culture. I don't mean to imply these people are dissimulating out of expediency. I think rather that people have become insecure about opening up in contact with others. The most common fears are that it will make us vulnerable, that others will not pardon our mistakes, and that we will leave a poor impression with the other person that would be difficult or impossible to correct. We could be rebuffed or even abandoned by the other person. We could learn that we weren't important to the other person and have been deluded in our perception of their friendliness and attention to us. But besides protecting ourselves against disappointment, the fear of fulfilment often plays a major role, perhaps even more often than the fear of disappointment. Or as Oscar Wilde put it in *Lady Windermere's Fan*: "In this world there are only two tragedies. One is not getting what one wants, and the other is getting it."

A young man came to me for treatment because he was afraid of encountering the female sex. He had good social contacts at his university, was popular and well respected. What he was lacking for happiness was a girlfriend. But that's where he failed. In the analytical process, we found out he was afraid of rejection and the loss of his reputation—he feared being thrown out of the university as a predator. He was unable to work on this matter as his fears only intensified. I decided to assign him a task intended to release him from his inner predicament: He was to approach four female students in the cafeteria and ask them out. Not until he had done that would I give him any more sessions. He soon came back. None of the students had reacted in a gruff or dismissive way. On the contrary, all had been pleased. The first three were in serious relationships and wanted to avoid entanglements. The fourth gave the patient her phone number. When I asked him whether he'd already arranged a date, he confessed with a downcast gaze that he'd forgotten the piece of paper with the phone number in the cafeteria. This also made him realize how frightened he was of fulfilling his heart's desire.

The young man was not primarily concerned with sexuality but with closeness to a loved one. That's what he was afraid of, since the fourth student apparently had this need, too.

Now, one could easily attribute this plight to clinical causes, which are certainly responsible at times for a reluctance about closeness. For the majority of people, however, there are other causes. Not only have we lost our capacity for closeness, but we have also developed a discomfort with closeness, even a fear of it.

At first sight, the fear and caution arising from this may seem paradoxical.

2.5 Dealing with others

What we inflict on others comes back to us

Tenzin Wankshuk comes to me excitedly: "The Lama said you should come to him today. For tea." The lama ... which lama? Oh, right, up there in the gompa. I feel somewhat blindsided, but also a bit guilty. Should I have known? Should I have requested an audience with the lama? Have I committed a serious faux pas? I can't bring him anything. I've left my last khata, the customary gift of a white scarf for a Buddhist dignitary, with a head lama, whose name I have unfortunately forgotten. I can't give this lama anything. Except my time. "Does the lama speak Ladakhi?" I want to know from Tenzin. "No, only Urdu." Our interpreter on this research trip speaks only Ladakhi, and his English is at least as bad as mine. He is a student of electrical engineering in Srinagar. And he has a gift for destroying moods. It's an excellent opportunity not to take that pain in the neck with us.

Tashi Tsering stands at the top of the parapet of his gompa. With what appears like serene detachment, he observes how we Western Europeans pant our way up the steep path. At the top he welcomes us with a bow. He invites us into a room we would probably call a living room. There's a table here and an unbelievable view over the Zanskar valley. Tashi Tsering returns from the kitchen with a large kettle of steaming tea. As he pours it, I relax: no butter tea. It's a delicacy in the Himalayas, but not for my stomach. I would have been very embarrassed had I thrown up this delicacy at the door of his gompa. Tashi Tsering opens a box of biscuits. We drink the tea, nibble the biscuits, and look out the window. We don't exchange a word the whole time. We don't even look at each other. And yet there is no onerous feeling. The lama suddenly stands up and signals with his hand that it's getting dark soon and we'd better leave while it's still light out. We say goodbye with an exchange of bows. The lama was right; it did get dark quickly.

On the way down, Tenzin Wankshuk and his son Dorshe are already coming toward us with paraffin lamps. We go to him. We eat chapatis and drink tea. Suddenly, there is a knock at the door. Tashi Tsering, the lama, is at the door. I am completely mystified. What is it, I want to know from our host father. The lama holds a half-full plastic bottle of water out to me that we'd forgotten at the gompa.

But that wasn't necessary, I try to indicate. Yes, it was, Tenzin Wankshuk insists. Otherwise, it would have resulted in bad karma. A water bottle costs five rupees, which is about five cents. And Tashi Tsering came without a lamp.

One may believe in rebirth or not. The lama does. Or maybe he just wants to play it safe in case it's true. In the Buddhist faith, similar here to the Christian faith, it's important that the balance between good and bad actions be right; it plays a significant role for the next life. The balance, that is, between actions that have harmed others and those that have been good for others. On the Christian side, a divine authority decides where one may live in the afterlife, but in Buddhism it seems to be a law. Those who have accumulated a lot of good—or even solely good—on their "karma account" may hope to be reborn as a human being. Perhaps even in a better position, as a lama, a Rinpoche, or as the Dalai Lama.

Those who end up with a bad account balance, perhaps even a negative one, are reborn as animals or insects or worms. You've already guessed what the order is. In this new life, he must again collect points in his reincarnated form. Try that as a cockroach! Though they're actually quite nice animals. They may not look swanky, but they eat only as much as they need, they don't spread diseases, and they will survive nuclear war. If we contrast this with humans: We "eat" (or collect) more than we need, spread diseases, and invented nuclear war. Our only remaining asset is our better appearance (from the human point of view).

I maintain, and my experiences prove me right, that everything we "do" to others bounces back to us. I asked Tamara, a good friend, how I could ever compensate her. Tamara helped me when I went through a difficult time. I couldn't have made it without her. Tamara said quite modestly: "I don't need anything; I have everything I need; I'm happy. Help someone else who really needs help, like you did then. It will somehow come back to me. I believe," she confided to me in a softer voice, "that we are all connected. And even if it travels around the world once, it will eventually come back to me." A few years later she met a great man, just the right man, a gem of a man. That was the one thing she was still missing.

Should you not be so mystically inclined: For one thing, others sense our inner stance. We sense whether the car salesman is honest, whether we've come across well at our job interview, whether someone is a rascal or a scoundrel, whether the nice man who just spoke to us is only looking for a quick fling. On the other hand, actions also shape our character. At some point you sense, and you do so more clearly over time, whether someone takes his fellow human beings seriously or just wants to use or exploit them, whether he's just a taker, not a giver.

Melanie Klein, a well-known Austrian-British psychoanalyst, once coined the term "good object." By this she means an inner entity of someone's personality that is well-disposed toward him- or herself and also toward others. It values and protects the weak; it helps when necessary. We humans bring this inner good object along as a seed at birth, as well as its opposite: the evil object. It's up to us which plant we water and nurture and which we let wither. The task of psychoanalysis is to rediscover, unfetter, or revive the good object in the human being. Incidentally, one of the reasons I became a psychoanalyst and psychotherapist is because it allows me to engage with the good object throughout my life.

Those who do good make their good object flourish. I am not talking about altruistic renunciation here. But I'm neither a utilitarian hedonist nor a follower of Epicurus. I am not even an academic—a peripatetic probably fits me best. I'm suspicious of simple solutions. I prefer to treat life as a quest.

3. Feelings

3.1 Affection

At first, it may seem obvious that we need the love of other people. There's no doubt some truth in that. In my experience, however, the love of others is a double-edged sword. What is quite clear: We want to be seen and perceived by others. Not only do we want to be seen in our existence, but we long for the feeling of having a firm place in this world. And we want to be important to others. Not only to have a place in the community, but to be useful to it or to individuals in it. Indeed, we help willingly. The reward for helping is to experience that the other person is better off. That he or she is perhaps freed of an ill, a predicament, or a dilemma. The feeling of helping is very similar to the feeling of giving a gift to another person. The giver is the actual recipient of the gift, as he or she can enjoy the other person's joy. Declining help often causes the same hurt as rejecting a gift. Even more: I think helping others is the most beautiful gift that people can give others.

Nevertheless, there's a qualification here. Usually, we always help, as much as we can. But we do not always do it with the same dedication. If an offer of help is refused that we've made purely out of a sense of obligation, we're often glad that we've been spared the trouble. For there is an essential difference in the quality of relationships that we'll look at in the next chapter.

But first, I want to return to the question of whether we need the love of others. This remains a difficult question to answer, but one thing is certain: We need the attention of others. However, it seems to me that the love of others is not without danger. It's too easily associated with mirror gazing or a lack of self-esteem—a phenomenon we call narcissism. The love of others can easily become an addiction. The narcissist needs it to have his grandiosity constantly mirrored, just as a person lacking in self-esteem needs it to get any appreciation whatsoever.

In what other ways can love be dangerous? For this, we have to look at our early childhood. Humans are born prematurely. Our brains are so big that birth would not be workable if we were fully grown. We humans have two accidental genetic mutations to thank for this fact. Five million years ago, the gene ARHGAP 11A mutated into the gene ARHGAP 11B. The new gene results in a higher cell doubling rate. At first, nothing happened because the gene was in the wrong place—until a million years ago, when the new gene moved into the mitochondria of the brain cells. Since then, the human brain has been growing unremittingly. The rest hasn't kept pace; the uterus and pelvis weren't able to adapt in the brief frame of time, so a premature birth was the only possible solution in the evolution of humankind.

This is why young people need the "social womb," as described by the gifted researcher of children's relationships with their mothers, Margaret Mahler (1980). Young children need the security and safety of maternal and paternal love to develop "primal trust," a term coined by the developmental researcher Erik H. Erikson (1966). Primal trust develops through the loss of the fear of being left alone, which would mean death for the infant; it grows by experiencing stable affection, where people feel safe, cherished, and secure. But there is a flip side. We must come out of the physical womb, and we also have to and want to come out of our social womb. We want to develop, to explore the world and ourselves. To try things out and to improve. Curiosity and the irrepressible urge to develop and grow are engines that drive oneself, and ultimately humanity, forward. Not that the latter is guaranteed, of course: developments, discoveries, or inventions can also, as we know, cause harm. Too much love can be dangerous; the love of so-called helicopter parents can become an extreme impediment because it reinforces "natural" childlike insecurity and leaves the child believing that there's much she cannot manage on her own. These children might as well start saving for a psychiatrist.

We want to explore and develop throughout our lives. However, this will not succeed if we stay in the nest. As soon as an infant can crawl, he can hardly be stopped. Once a child can climb and open drawers, she will clearly show her determination to make this world her own.

3.2 Loneliness and devotion

We suffer from loneliness because we don't feel secure. This may lead to the conclusion that we only suffer because we need the love and security of other people. However, we know from loneliness research that people suffer even more when they can't give others love and security. This was discovered by the American loneliness researcher Robert Weiss (1975). Even without research, everyday experience shows this to be true when we consider how many lonely people get pets to care for affectionately. And it needn't always be cats or dogs, animals which, you could say, return our affection. For many, it can be fish, insects, or reptiles, even disgusting, dangerous, or poisonous animals with which any form of physical affection would be unpleasant or fatal. Nevertheless, animal lovers devote themselves to the care of these animals with great love and dedication. It needn't even be a relationship with a particular animal; a connection can be formed with a species or genus, as is the case with animal welfare activists who advocate for wildlife in the forests. Often, they don't even get to see these creatures. I once did an experiment with my son. We hung up a bird nesting box and installed a small camera in it. Not just my son, but all the observers swooned over the live transmission of the incubation, the hatching of the birds, but above all the tender feeding—even though the picture was only in black and white.

Giving love is an essential basic need for us humans. If it's not fulfilled, we suffer. Caring for, indulging, "feeding," and supporting other people gives us great satisfaction and bestows on us moments of happiness again and again, while denial or deprivation of caring makes us suffer greatly. One could almost say our soul hungers to give others affection.

This need, alongside other, often less pleasant qualities, not only accounts for the success of the human species but has ultimately ensured our survival. If we didn't enjoy giving love more than harming others, we would probably have eradicated each other with sticks and stones in prehistoric times.

3.3 Closeness

Our reserve about closeness can have pathological causes. After early disappointment in or abuse of a child's desire for closeness, the hurt person wants to protect himself from being hurt or disappointed again. He or she likely must do so because otherwise they're sucked into a vortex of self-abjection from which they can't emerge on their own.

Interestingly, however, the reserve about closeness is also found in most healthy people. I do not, of course, expect an insensitive lack of distance in them so much as a kind of natural opposite. Closeness, be it emotional or physical, requires the other person's consent.

What I mean here is a reserve about the need itself, or more precisely, of permitting the need. We're no longer able to, in a natural way, take these needs seriously and give them space. Why isn't it possible nowadays to simply say to someone: "May I sit with you for a while?" "Yes, why?" "Oh, just because you seem very likeable." Surely that should at least flatter most people. But, of course, one isn't always in the mood for contact. Sometimes you just want—or need—some peace and quiet. And on the other hand, the person you're talking to doesn't dare say: "I'm very flattered. But excuse me, I need some time for myself right now. Maybe later." Superficially, it appears to be a fear of embarrassment—but I think it's more fear of rejection. And behind that lies our fear of being disappointed in others and thus feeling rage. That explains part of our self-inhibited caution. But there are other causes for our inhibition. In a positive sense, we could cite respect for the other person's self-determination and privacy. This can be honored, however, by asking the other person for permission, and giving him or her the option of refusal from the outset. And by my accepting it, as a strong character, without anger or thoughts of revenge, with a simple "too bad," and with the right to try again, unless the other person has clearly signaled they want no contact at all.

A final rejection, breaking off contact, or a ban on contact strikes a deep-seated nerve in us. It's not only the personal injury. Exclusion immediately touches on primal existential fears. In the evolutionary depths of our existence, being excluded from the community is tantamount to a death sentence. An agonizing death, being forced to starve in loneliness, helplessly exposed to all manner of dangers without the community's protection. This is stored in our brain stem and generates those existential fears that, when assessed soberly or from the outside, appear grossly exaggerated.

Incidentally, the same fears are aroused in an infant when its mother is absent and doesn't respond to his or her cries for help, or, by the child's standards, responds with too long a delay. They're also aroused in love relationships. When one party leaves or is about to end the relationship, people in our culture usually react as if their lives are directly threatened, as if they could not exist without the other, even though they may have already been coping well for years or decades with an autonomous, independent life. Suddenly they react like children and can no longer be reached with factual arguments or reassurances. This is understandable: The fear program in the brain stem has been activated.

Why is that? Why do people in our culture react so strongly? I deliberately say "our culture" because I've not experienced this in communal cultures. The reason is our particular, culturally-shaped relationship with our mother. When we're still helpless and the world seems (and is) unmanageable and impossible to cope with, we need a psychologically stable mother who senses our needs and understands our utterances, a mother who can protect us, nurture us, and keep us alive. "Mother" stands here for an important function of protection, security, and safety. This task can be taken on by different genders and by more than one person. In our culture, it's usually taken over by one particular person, which results in a dangerous dependency in various respects or, as the case may be, at different points in our human development. If there's only one person ensuring our survival, we're at great risk. We must not lose that person. We must not anger that person. Otherwise, our brain stem — our biological operating system, in somewhat modern terms — signals to us that we may be in mortal danger. Our rational mind has no opportunity to object to this. Our primal instincts have taken control.

In so-called communal cultures, the bond to one person, namely to the biological mother, isn't as strong. Here, in most cases, all the women of a village take on the mothering task I've described. The child gets a "village mother." And it's quite difficult, if not impossible, to antagonize an entire village community. That's how I experienced it, for example, with the Ovahimba in Namibia. In their language, the term "mother" stands for the person who carried and delivered the child. Since Ovahimba aren't familiar with ownership, there's no such thing in relation to children — or partners. Children don't belong to anyone; they're raised by the whole village. A mother can simply leave the village and her child behind. If he cries, another mother will immediately come and comfort or breastfeed him. No one would condemn her as a bad mother or blame her, let alone call the youth welfare office on her. The mother, after all, belongs to no one, not even her child. Everyone belongs to themselves. As relates to partnerships, this leads to great sexual permissiveness among the Ovahimba. Why shouldn't my neighbor be allowed to sleep with my wife? After all, I hold him in high esteem. And mutual respect plays a big role among the Ovahimba. Due to these circumstances, women among the Ovahimba have the greatest possible sexual self-determination, which ensures them a varied sexual diet and permits curiosity about new experiences. This poses an enormous challenge for the Western researcher's self-control: Sexual rejection is equated with personal rejection. Ovahimba don't understand that the chemistry may not be right, or the spark simply doesn't catch on. The sexual "no" remains an affront. I've always used religious reasons as an excuse: I'm having a sexual fasting period, and my God would react very badly. That always works. By the way, it also works when you're offered fresh maggots, warm cow's blood, or goat's eyes. "Thank you, I would love to try, but delicacies are forbidden during Lent."

In our culture, children are considered their parents' property and, conversely, parents are considered their children's property. Our partners belong to us and we to them. Many people will strongly resist the idea because officially everyone is "free," but unofficially they are each other's property. This also explains why many people experience themselves as "possessions" of their society, and strive for the greatest possible freedom and self-determination, while at the same time protecting themselves against heteronomy.

The kind of bond that exists in communal cultures—a bond which equally honors community and freedom—has been lost here. Because of that, a bond must always be bought with promises and obligations. The Zanskari, a people living in the second Himalayan range in villages above 3,500 meters (I gave an account of them above), were bewildered when I mentioned to them the restriction of freedom by the community in my society. Why restrictions? Can't everyone do what they want? They didn't understand the question of whether self-centered behavior could lead to conflicts with others or with the village community, or even cause harm. Was it not a matter of course that people behaved respectfully? Where did I get such an idea? When I told them self-centered behavior was customary among us, the Zanskari just shook their heads to express their incomprehension. For them, there are no obligations, only matters of course.

I didn't tell them that in Western cultures we teach self-centeredness and self-actualization and place a focus on them as a high goal of human freedom and development, and that ruthlessness, egoism, and elbowing are not only condoned, but encouraged. I feared being thrown out of the village. And rightly so, because such things simply don't belong in a human community. Perhaps it was just my deep desire to throw ruthlessness, selfishness, and elbowing out of our society. If there were a trapdoor through which to dispose of these scourges of humanity, I would've pulled the lever long ago.

In Western cultures, individual needs have come to be seen as incompatible with an equitable existence and mutual respect. "You and we" has given way to "I or the others." Altruism is increasingly giving way to the selfishness of the stronger or smarter. Altruism has become parasitism. People gladly accept the amenities of a society, the services of hospitals, fire departments, and day-care centers, but prefer to pay their taxes in a tax haven—and are even admired for this cleverness. Nurses, whose salaries aren't commensurate with what they provide, are an exception. In my opinion, and as an aside, taxes should be adjusted to the value that the individual's service has for the community. Nurses and educators would thus pay no taxes in my ideal country. The shortfalls created would be filled by shareholders or entrepreneurs like Jeff Bezos. And I would have no sympathy were Mr. Bezos to be taxed at 98 percent. He would still be left with two billion net. To put the amount in perspective: For that, you would have to get six numbers right in the weekly German lottery every Saturday for twenty-five and a half years. Looking at it from the other side: Mr. Bezos could still "squander" five and a half million a day. But now he has quit and can retire with two hundred billion. If we grant him a hundred years of life, he will have four and a half billion per year as his "pension," meaning he could spend close to thirteen million a day.

Nevertheless, he is admired in our culture. And many would likely be startled by the idea of taxing him at 98 percent rather than just 1 percent, as is the reality. Presumably, Jeff Bezos would also see it that way. "My beautiful billions are gone," he would perhaps lament, rather than driving past the town's new fire station and rejoicing in the fact that his money too is in there. Or enabling 66 million children to get a solid, school education. Or saving 333 million children from starvation for ten years.

Human values have long been cheapened in our culture. Officially, they're held in high esteem, but secretly, the clever tax evader, whom the law doesn't regard as such because he avails himself of loopholes, is more admired — not least because this creates distance to the weak or needy and avoids closeness and compassion. Anyone who observes a child at an Indian rubbish dump looking for something to eat will immediately feel close to this child and never forget the image. After that, the irritation that Amazon can only deliver my laptop adapter the day after tomorrow becomes an embarrassing farce.

Let us turn to dependency and possession-centered thinking to reflect on another cause of our reserve about closeness. Our caution is also based on a need for freedom, which, in our culture, seems to collide with closeness and attachments or relationships. Three other causes are significant here. Firstly, the feeling of obligation already referred to can trigger resistance that we call reactance. Secondly, dependence on one's mother binds us in a unique way beyond the time that's biologically necessary. In the phase when a toddler is exploring the world, wanting to make it and his own body his own, this becomes a problem. This is where the mother, who in our culture is often overprotective, interferes. Among the Zanskari, I saw small children running at such a great height that I had to pause for a moment in shock. The adults weren't concerned at all. They just laughed at me. If they only knew that in this country, for many parents, even a two-meter-high slide poses a potential danger to their child's life and limb!

This well-intentioned overprotectiveness hinders a child's individual development, leads to basic mistrust in her own abilities on the child's part, and to an ambivalence toward her mother, who wants to prevent the child from expanding. The child has to free herself from this.

But that's not all that makes closeness seem so suspect. All humans long for the feeling of security in their early years. Some colleagues believe that one's time in the womb plays a special role in this. Many songs, but also great novels, are about a deep longing. We don't really know what is being longed for, but everyone knows the feeling, for example, of melancholy entering one's heart upon seeing the beaming eyes of one's own child looking at the Christmas tree. One remembers the paradise of the past, which is irretrievably lost. It can only be preserved in one's imagination and the yearning desires for it expressed in songs, novels, or films. This fact was already understood in the bible: As soon as we have eaten from the tree of knowledge, we must leave paradise. To develop, knowledge is necessary, and expulsion from paradise inevitable--unless one wants to live in a psychosis all one's life. This, then, points to the third cause for our reserve about closeness. In Greek mythology, Epimetheus wants to remain in the paradise of non-development in childlike naivety, but he eventually opens

Pandora's box, the Greek equivalent of the apple from the tree of knowledge. His brother Prometheus, evidently the more adult and rational one, recognizes the danger and, to minimize the damage, steals fire from the gods. In both genesis stories, disobeying one's parents is necessary for human development. This is a process I have defined as "positioning oneself toward one's parents." In psychology, we often speak of "letting go" or "detachment," but I consider this term a distortion, because we never truly detach ourselves from our parents. Even if they have long since died, they remain important, essential components of our personality. With the positioning, parents are retained as inner objects— only our relationship to them changes.

3.4 Thoughts versus feelings

The power of thoughts and the powerlessness of feelings

At the beginning of human evolution, setting aside whether it was four million years or two million years or just a hundred thousand years ago, there were only feelings. Feelings are biologically determined reactions, chains of reactions, or entire biological programs. They are the same in all people at the beginning of life. Later, they're shaped in positive terms by our socialization and support, but also by education, manipulation, and the bending or even gutting of our personality, in negative terms. Feelings differ from thoughts in that they're not malleable and can't immediately be corrected, especially since they're usually accompanied or triggered by a physiological reaction. It's possible to supplant one feeling with another, as parents often try to do to distract a child, though this is a form of manipulating children's moral rights. But one can't correct feelings as one can an illogical thought, or an incorrect mathematical calculation. Feelings defy logic. "The guy is not worth crying your eyes out about!" — may well be true, but saying so will not make the forsaken woman feel less distraught.

Thoughts are the attempt to interrupt the immediacy of the reactions following feelings and to deconstruct and then reconstruct the situation that set one off—free of feelings and emotions, and, above all, free of fear. Instead of running away from the fire, it can make sense to head directly toward it, preferring the risk of burn injuries to being suffocated by smoke in a dead end. A special form of reasoned action was introduced in air travel in the late 1980s and 1990s. In an emergency, rather than hectically spinning around and yelling hysterically, as is often shown in American disaster films, pilots carry out a situation check especially developed for emergency situations called FOR-DEC. The individual letters specify the tasks and the order in which they're to be completed. At the same time, wisely, the hierarchy between captain and co-pilot was done away with: both fly the plane; one steers while the other monitors the instruments. Who does what is determined beforehand. This may cost more time than reactive, off-the-cuff action, but you can't afford many failed attempts in the air. This is a sensible and necessary development of human rationality. Emotions have no place in the cockpit, especially when things get dicey. This is intended only as an example; I don't intend to idealize feelings and condemn rationality.

We humans like to claim we discovered reason and thinking. This is not strictly true. In the Arctic, for example, there are species of seal that have developed a preliminary stage of thinking. They're able to suppress their "natural" fight-or-flight reflex as a reaction, for example, to their fear of an approaching polar bear. Instead of fleeing frantically, they hide behind an iceberg and try not to make a sound. It's not that they "thought this up"; it came about through trial and error. Or natural selection: Those who fled got caught, those who didn't survived.

Our evolutionary relatives, chimpanzees and other great apes, are capable of more complex thought processes.

Experiments have shown, for example, that they can create one long tube by sticking several tubes together; with it, they can fish for a banana hanging from the ceiling that seems to be out of reach for them. Our species, however, is the only one known thus far to develop these simple thought processes to unprecedented precision and effectiveness. We no longer need real poles; we can put them together in our imagination, in our heads. We can even mentally construct (i.e., invent) objects that don't exist yet. We can think through different possible reactions, tell others about them and discuss them so that they too think about them. Freud called it "action in rehearsal," and gave this type of thinking the name "secondary process thinking," juxtaposing it against feelings, which he called "primary process thinking."

The form of secondary process thinking is already very old. Without this form of thinking, the pyramids or other wonders of the world wouldn't have been possible. Nor would early seafaring, certainly. A ship that can sail from Norway to America can't be made by trial and error.

Sciences such as mathematics, physics, astronomy, medicine, and psychology wouldn't have come into being without "emotionless" thinking.

Interestingly, this thinking was mainly used for technical or scientific findings and developments. Even psychology only discovered feelings as an object of research at a very late stage.

The Reformation and the era of Enlightenment led to a close questioning of human fears. Particularly in the scope of religion and the church, fears were often used for manipulation and to suppress certain groups or individuals, or at least to keep them in their place. Unfortunately, oppression continues to exist, but thanks to the Reformation and the era of Enlightenment we can also free ourselves from many fears. Hardly anyone fears purgatory anymore, although in the Middle Ages many smart people were burned at the stake for exposing the manipulation of religious fears as scientific nonsense. The consequence of the Enlightenment wasn't only a disempowerment of the nobility and the church, but also a strengthening of the sciences, which were explicitly promoted and called upon. Science works best without feelings. A physicist who shoots two atoms at each other to break them down into their constituent parts ought not to have any compassion for either. Objectivity was required. Feelings became more and more a side effect of certain situations or circumstances, one that wasn't always desired, like flatulence after eating legumes.

This is the prevailing state of affairs today. Feelings have some justification, but their form and intensity should be in our hands. Preferably, they should be as controllable as the FOR-DEC procedure mentioned above. Programs on the internet calculate which partner suits us best. This is done with algorithms that retrieve preferences, inclinations, dislikes, wishes, hobbies, leisure interests, and so on that have been queried beforehand. But how is an emotionless computer program supposed to determine which person does me good? Let's say I end up with an archery-loving, Mozart-loving pescetarian who likes to take vacations in Mexico, likes to read books by Frank Schätzing and Stephen King, but despises crime series on TV. Let's say, not that you should take my word for this unquestioningly, there's a match of 98 percent. I should marry this woman right then and there. But it becomes difficult if there are *two* matches: one matching 99.5 percent and the other 99.6 percent. Rationally speaking, the second one would be the better choice. You see what nonsense this is. Because the decisive factor between two people is not congenial interests or the lack of conflicts when choosing a movie or a restaurant, but whether feelings develop between the two. If we're attracted to a person, we would not first ask him whether he too likes to listen to jazz music, especially by Cannonball Adderley, and loves hiking on the island of Fuerteventura or movies starring Liam Neeson. The conversation would certainly be very short: he or she would think we've a serious screw loose. We also don't look at whether and how this person smiles, but *feel* what we feel when he or she smiles. Does this not sound better already? A crucial factor in the question of whether we're compatible is the feelings we have when we see the other person, when we're waiting for them, when we lie in their arms or hear their voice. But all of this is difficult to grasp scientifically — in my opinion, it can't be done at all. Is it the "right pressure" the other person uses when they hug us, the pitch of their voice that fascinates us, or perhaps the angle at which they look us in the eye? It's a mixture of all kinds of factors. According to the latest research, the optimal fit between one's immune systems is decisive for whether a partnership comes together. One's unconscious can recognize this by odor. That's possible, but who cares? It's possible the unconscious says no to a potential partner if the immune systems do not suit each other.

But, after all, we don't come together as couples primarily to produce "optimal offspring" for posterity, but to have a good time together. And for that, neither a fit between immune systems nor a fit in other things suffices. Whether feelings arise and, if so, which ones, cannot be predicted or controlled. We can prepare ourselves for a meeting with a potential partner by dressing nicely. Even if we're charming, witty, and intelligent in our conversation, we can't influence whether sparks will fly. But we can feel whether something is developing. Even if, to our regret, this isn't the case.

And that's a good thing, too. Feelings can and should be surprises from our unconscious. I'm sure that Google, if I were to use that data-stealing machine, could relieve me of many decisions rather precisely on the basis of the data it has collected about me. (Or, rather, that I have—voluntarily—supplied to Google!) Maybe, one day, even all my decisions. Google would choose the right profession for me, a suitable university, the perfect tennis racket, and probably also the best tennis club. It would plan my vacations for me, select the right wine, and so forth. A truly unsettling idea.

When my son bought his first smartphone, he proudly showed me an app in which he can store, for example, offers from stores selling electronics. When he drives past one of those stores, the app informs him if the item is (still) available, and asks him whether the navigation system should lead him directly there. At least he's still being asked—at some point, his car will drive there on its own, the amount will be automatically debited from his credit card, and the item will be handed to him directly through his side window.

My son said that with this app, I would never miss an offer again. Admittedly, I'm enticed when, for example, an external hard drive costs only sixty euros rather than ninety euros. Thirty euros saved. But I do it in the conventional way: I cut out these offers, put them on my desk, and throw them away when it's time to tidy up—expired three weeks ago. I'm not annoyed, because it wasn't an app that decided for me, but my unconscious: Apparently, the bargain wasn't that important to me. And I'm happy—I didn't save just thirty euros, but sixty! Sometimes, I make it even easier for myself: I no longer cut out the offers, but rather throw them straight away, and I'm immediately happy about the money I've saved. I feel the same way about Black Friday. I always miss out on it because I know the only products offered are ones you don't need. But they are offered at half price, which is why you go ahead and take two of them.

Recently, I was walking through Berlin with my son and we got hungry. There are many restaurants in Berlin. He pulled out his smartphone and announced there were three restaurants in the immediate vicinity: a Persian one, a Greek one, and an Italian one. Which would I prefer? Actually, I'd hoped he would surprise me with a personal insider tip. I don't know why, but something always inspires me: the Greek place there looks kind of good. A quick look at the menu: souvlaki, great, maybe a samos or Mavrodaphne to go with it. No problem, each of these restaurants has a website with its menu. You can even visit the Persian restaurant virtually and book a table. At the thought that the food too might already be placed on the tables, I gave up. My patience had run out, and my hunger had reached an almost unbearable level. Fortunately, a curry sausage stand appeared out of nowhere. Without a website, without an app, we ordered original Berlin currywurst and ate it standing at the kiosk. It was delicious.

I want to choose a restaurant myself. I want to read the menu, ask what the delicious-looking dish at the next table is, whether they recommend it. And then hungrily devour the pieces of bread with butter or curd cheese and gorge myself on the food when it finally arrives.

Feelings are the most important thing in our experience because everything we remember is interwoven with feelings. We attach feelings to everything — objects, memories, activities, people, even abstract concepts like the future, god, hope, the New Year, and so on (the fancy psychoanalytical term for this is cathexis). But we also do this with things we don't know yet, such as a tourist destination we haven't been to but intend to visit, and even with people we don't know personally, like celebrities or the Dalai Lama. He is widely popular, and perhaps a thorn only in the side of hardliners in the Chinese government. But how do we know if his gentleness is just an act, and he's actually an angry fellow? I can assure you he isn't. In fact, he's quite a mischievous person who likes to have some fun in private.

There are positive, negative, and neutral cathexes, or casts of mind. The neutral ones are all things, places, activities that we don't know, with which we have no experience. When you imagine the country of Zambia, what do you feel? Maybe you think of samba and get warm feelings, thinking of the music. Or you get negative feelings, because, despite private dance lessons, you still haven't mastered the whole thing. But Zambia probably doesn't trigger any feelings. On the other hand, a police radar device probably does. And a letter from the tax office even more so. If you were expecting a hefty tax bill but find out when you read it that you'll be getting an unexpected refund, your cast of mind changes abruptly.

Without feelings, our lives would be boring and lifeless. Just imagine a crime thriller that shows only boring police work. No entanglements, no guessing "whodunnit." Or a football match without emotions—who would watch something like that?

3.5 Sensuality

The loss of sensuality and why it's a basic need

The fate of sensuality has something in common with the fate of feelings: it too is decreasing more and more. Like feelings, it is being marginalized by rationality. Perhaps this is because sensuality is also a feeling—or multiple feelings simultaneously. Ultimately, it doesn't matter which. I believe we need sensuality for our well-being.

First, we should consider what sensuality actually is. I take sensuality to mean the perception or the experience of an event with a particular devotion or depth of the involved senses, to the exclusion of other senses and perceptions, but above all to the exclusion of (conscious) thoughts and other activities. When a flower we sniff smells particularly good, so that we want to perceive the whole thing even more intensely and breathe the scent in again, perhaps bringing our nose closer to the pistils, we are not considering what individual smells are coming together there, what plant species it is, or whether the scent is meant to attract certain insects. Rather, feelings are evoked in us, and sometimes images or memories as well. On a gray winter day when you feel irritable, open a bottle of sunscreen and breathe the smell in deeply. Immediately, your mood will brighten. Images of the beach come to mind, perhaps of a particular beach. You'll probably want to inhale the smell again—and then pore through a travel brochure. The sense of smell is our "oldest" sense, though we no longer necessarily need it today. It's the one best linked to our memory system—for both positive and negative associations. Smell a bottle of Focaldry, that disinfectant dentists often use, should you have one in the house. I need say no more. You definitely wouldn't go out and buy that product.

But our other senses are also capable of perceiving a variety of impressions. You can hardly smell or hear a sunset, but perhaps you associate the visual sensation with a typical smell of seaweed and the sound of the sea. If you drink a good red wine while doing so, your sense of taste will also be activated; perhaps, together with the red wine, a pleasurable feeling will spread in your stomach. Should you be lying in a nice person's arms, your feeling of well-being is perfect.

Unfortunately, only smells can be preserved astonishingly well. A photo of the sunset cannot even begin to recreate the visual sensory quality. Probably, the same red wine will still taste good to us, but somehow different. The discrepancy of decoupling sensory experiences can be observed with music in particular. You're probably familiar with the phenomenon: The fado CD by a music group, which so enchanted you at the Rossio in Lisbon, doesn't have the same effect back home in your living room. Fado has faded.

Should you now say that you don't know sensuality, or no longer know it, that you "don't have the time" or "the guts" for sensuality, it's high time to think about whether — and, above all, how — you can bring sensuality back.

Sensuality is not a new discovery made by civilized human beings. It's the oldest form of experience and originates from the pre-linguistic times of mankind. That's why it's the best and healthiest form of pleasure. And it's not the most expensive. Certainly, a trip to Lisbon does not come cheaply, and a Mediterranean vacation also costs you money.

But just because it's the most "innocent," purest form of perception, feeling, and experience, it need not cost much. We need only look to our children. They experience everything impartially, want to smell and feel and experience everything with all their senses; they are completely immersed in doing so. Anyone who walks through a forest for an hour with a toddler who has just learned to walk will be able to witness the zeal with which a beetle can be observed during a 300-meter walk. Or a caterpillar slowly climbing along a branch. Even stones and sticks acquire such a sensual quality that they must be taken along — the parents among my readers will know what I'm talking about. Of course, caterpillars, snails, and beetles should also be taken along. For the toddlers, a treat, for many parents, a way to improve their frustration tolerance. And, even better, to reclaim their sensuality.

Over time, children unlearn their sensuality. All children like to paint because it's such a beautiful, sensual experience. Feeling how your own hand guides the brush and enjoying how it feels when the brush skims over the paper with the paint. The smell of the paint. Or, when finger painting, the slippery feeling of your hands, the sound when you slap the paper — or the living room wall. The feeling when the paint dries on the palm of your hand, or, even better, your whole naked body is covered with paint, in itself already a very sensual experience. And then the warm water in the bathtub, the splashing and splattering, the sound of the water when it lands on the bathroom floor. The warm, soft sponge with soapy foam that my mother cleans me with. The funny games my father plays with the foam: the foam nose he gives me, the devil's horns he sometimes puts on my head. And we always laugh and have fun doing it. Then I'm dried off with the big terrycloth towel and wrapped up in my bathrobe. Sometimes I'm even allowed to fall asleep in my mom and dad's bed. In any event, they read a very interesting story aloud to me.

You smile, perhaps chuckle. You ask yourself how you could still do that today, now that you're an adult? Just try gently lathering your partner with a sponge. Or paint each other unclothed. There are special body paints, but I would advise against oil paint.

Creative therapy is an integral feature at psychotherapeutic or psychosomatic clinics. The reason for this should be clear: they want to help patients regain and rediscover their sensuality.

We call it "regression in the service of the ego." A healthy form of activity that cavemen were already acquainted with some 37,000 years ago. At first it was thought the drawings in Chauvet Cave were made to teach children, like the drawings in Twyfelfontein or Okonguarri in Namibia. Then it was discovered the animals depicted were not prey, nor did the drawings show dangers that people needed to be warned about. Ecco: People back then already painted "simply for sensual pleasure."

Unfortunately, many people find it relatively easy to give up their sensuality, and they find it very difficult to recapture it later. Let's take a closer look at why this is.

First, I'll give an example. A patient came to see me because he'd had panic attacks after his daughter was born. He found no reason for them. He was a smart, educated man, successful in his career, popular in his private life. He lived in a healthy partnership. We discovered the cause when the patient said he no longer dared to go into the forest with his daughter. What had happened? Had the two of them had a disturbing experience? No, he feared he would no longer be able to find his way out of the forest because he would forget the time and not go home. But he had a mobile phone, surely his wife would call at some point.

His fear was more deeply seated. He'd completely fused with his daughter's sensual exploration. He'd forgotten space and time. He'd forgotten himself, probably even his name—in short, everything that was not necessary at the moment, perhaps even detrimental. He was completely focused, but not in a concentrated sense. Instead, he'd let himself drift. And what was even more dangerous in his eyes, he enjoyed it. He was drawn in, as he describes it, as if into a whirlpool. When I said, "How nice that you were able to enjoy it so," he sat up straight on the couch. His look told me that he feared I'd lost my mind. I added: "But just that— that's what's scaring you. That there's something inside you that you think you can't control. But that's not the whole truth. In reality, you're scared you don't want to control it, and that you can't get enough of it." His hitherto suppressed hunger for sensual regression had evidently become so great that the repressive mechanisms in his unconscious were no longer strong enough to lock it away. In his daughter, they'd been given an innocent accomplice. Thus, the patient got into a double dilemma: He knew it was important for his daughter's development to engage in such sensualities, and hoped to rescue himself by "playing along" (i.e., pretending he also found it interesting). Then he let himself be seduced, or rather, enchanted, and carried away by his daughter's childlike, curious abandon and rapture. However, it didn't feel to him like a relaxed raft ride on a calm river, but rather more like a ride on the Zambezi River within hearing of Victoria Falls.

It's precisely these irrational fears of healthy regression, of abandoning oneself to sensuality, that many people in our culture have; in my experience, this is preponderantly true in women. While they can often engage more easily in regression in the service of their children, when it comes to personal regression, many of them are helplessly at the mercy of their own inhibitions. Most often, external reasons are cited that supposedly make it impossible for them to do anything for themselves. "I never have time. And if I do, I'm too tired." Do the days of women have fewer hours? Of course not. Time is the only resource that is equally distributed among all people. The women (and men) with this problem would only have to take the time for themselves. When I then ask them to do so, they usually present to me fears they've concocted out of nowhere. Partners who would starve to death if they were to go away for a week. Or children who would irreparably degenerate physically and mentally from eating junk food for a weekend. These mothers are first given the task of doing something for themselves for one hour each day. To spend one hour just with themselves. It's forbidden to tidy up, plan the shopping, or chat with girlfriends. Though the latter may be relaxing, it's not a regression, not a sensual retreat. That's why I send them to the Rhine River, which traverses the city of Bonn. So there's no excuse. Their cell phone or books are also forbidden. It's best to leave your cigarettes at home, too. "You've already got everything you need with you," I tell them. "But what should I do?" many want to know. "Just watch the ships, that's all!" "For one hour?" "Yes, for an hour." For many, initially, this seems like preparatory training for hell (I suspect "modern hell" is not permanently overheated, but rather has everything a person could wish for—except wireless access). Eventually, though, they get there. Sometimes I tell patients who find the exercise particularly difficult that they need to stay patient: their body has already arrived, but their soul has not yet.

It costs patience to regain oneself, your liveliness and sensuality, and it requires confronting your own fears about doing so. In actual fact, this would not be necessary at all. We have functioning inner apparatuses that protect us and intervene at the right moment, usually before things get serious. In any case, I've never heard of anyone who died of hunger while painting or of thirst in the bathtub.

In short: These fears are unwarranted.

This brings us to consider two other quite modern topics: postponing—technically called procrastination, a term that's only good for speech therapy exercises—and chaos. Should you be hoping I will now reveal a few tricks of the trade on how you could defeat one or the other, or both, of them, or at least get a better grip on them, I'm going to have to disappoint you. Let me tell you something about the charm of the two unloved virtues.

Before doing so, however, I don't intend to conceal the fact that I too had to regain my sensuality. Art teachers spoiled my enjoyment in painting, and German teachers went out of their way to make me understand I was a hopeless case. In addition to my profession as a psychoanalyst, I always wanted to write; I wanted to become a published author. At some point, I got rid of all that nonsense. I don't mean to say I didn't benefit from the advice of experienced people. On the contrary, I have benefited from a lot of recommendations, especially those I didn't listen to.

It's better and healthier to listen to one's heart than to the hogwash others often try to sell us.

Today, writing is the greatest sensual experience for me that I can do alone. And I have to do it alone. I am then completely in another world. Anyone who disturbs me in the process will suffer dire consequences. You've been warned.

And that brings us to the next point.

3.6 Pleasure

Why food is so expensive in France and yet makes you richer

"You know that food costs twice as much here in France than it does in Germany? Don't you care?" I ask Pierre. My question has hit Pierre's passion nerve, should such a thing exist—but I'm sure Pierre has one, as do many other French people. He goes on: "You Germans always buy food in the supermarket and then stuff yourselves with all that cheap crud. Food is so important, for the palate, for the stomach, for the soul, for love, for friendship. But that doesn't seem to matter to you Germans." I get a bonus lesson in the culture of living—in fact I was already convinced, though I didn't disclose that to Pierre. I didn't want to deprive him of the pleasure of putting me under the spell of French eating culture. Quite frankly, too, I wanted to spend a day with him drifting in French style.

"When we French intend to cook, it starts in the morning. We go to the market. We have to see what we're cooking, we have to feel it, smell it, breathe it in. You know: Your soul eats along with you." We go to the market, Pierre stops at the first stall, starts to chat with the merchant, a middle-aged man in a gray smock and a faded corduroy hat. Where are the eggplants from? "From the immediate region, very fresh." "May I feel one?" "Bien sûr," the merchant says, and hands Pierre a big eggplant. Pierre examines it thoroughly. Then he nods: "It's good, give me two of them." "That's what I'm saying," the shopkeeper says, "I sell fresh produce. Neuf euros, s'il vous plaît." Pierre hands him a ten-euro bill with a straight face, without calculating or asking how much per kilo, and pockets the coin he gets back, sight unseen. And so it continues. There's meat and fish in the market hall next door. Pierre buys two large sea breams, and I can already imagine them on a plate sprinkled with almond flakes; my nose already is already tantalized by the buttery-sweet aroma. My mouth waters. Pierre must have sensed this. "Eh, voilà, good or not good? Well, what do you say, mon ami allemand?" I nod, and we've reached the end—not only of the market hall but also of our shopping tour. And I'm wiped out. But we're not going home. We're in France. We go to the bistro next to the market hall. Every market in France has a bistro. Don't hold me to it, but I'd like to believe it—and I'd recommend you do so too! There's a hectic bustle in the bistro. They also sell cigarettes, tobacco, roll-your-own paper, and newspapers. Lottery tickets can also be turned in there. "Come on, let's sit outside, it's too noisy in here." Pierre shakes his head. "Patrick, deux pastis, tout de suite," he shouts into the bistro. "Shall we eat something? The sandwiches with thon, with tuna, are pretty good." French bistros sell sandwiches; unlike the rest of French cuisine, they are merely "pretty good."

There we sit. The sandwich has dispelled my hunger, and the pastis infuses my brain with an airy lightness. Pierre lights up a Gauloise blue and takes a drag, drawing the smoke into his lungs as if his life depended on it, blows the smoke out with an "ah." "La facture, Patrick." I go to pull my wallet out, but Pierre puts his hand on mine assertively.

"Oh, non, you are my guest. The guest does not pay in France!"

Okay. Then he looks at me roguishly; his look tells me he's up to something. "Have you noticed? We forgot the most important thing!" I'm at a loss. We have everything, the vegetables, fish, crème fraîche; we even went to the oil shop next to the market, where Pierre bought a hazelnut oil mix with Armagnac—"for the salade!" We've got the "salade" too, of course. What are we still missing? Ha, his look says while I'm still in the dark, ha, gotcha! "So, what's the most important thing about the meal? Huh? The wine. But we haven't forgotten the wine, we'll buy it directly from the vintner." And then he smiles at me with a wink. "And we'll choose it very, very rigorously! I promise!" Tapping me on the thigh, he says "Allons-y! Let's go!" The wine purchase was just as sensual, full of relish, and expansive, but it did me in. I admit I was pretty drunk. Fortunately, Pierre was driving.

"Allons-y, Monsieur Didier," Pierre says to me. He has dragged me off to Gascony for a few days. There is really good wine here, not that "complete crap" from Baron Rothschild; he intends to buy Château de Cassaigne. "And you, too!" "What do you want me to do?" "Acheter le vin, bien sûr!" He won't take no for an answer—he's adamant. And, of course, he knows the "right" vintners. And in the evening, there'll be a "big surprise: you'll be amazed."

In the evening, after the wine tasting—which I will discreetly skip here—came the surprise. We set off. I'm hungry. "Très bien, me too," Pierre says triumphantly, not telling me where we're going. I know him well, and what should go wrong? We first drive along a big country road, then a small one, then an even smaller one. At the end, Pierre suddenly turns off onto a dirt road that winds up a mountain. There's really supposed to be food here? Or are we going to end up at an illegal distillery—and then in a drunken coma? Suddenly, out of nowhere, an old country house appears from behind some bushes. "Voilà!" And, again, I hear the triumph in Pierre's voice. "Huh?" I say in my Rhineland dialect, which means, "I can't see anything here. Are you sure this is the right place?" I can't even see whether the house is inhabited. If I didn't know Pierre so well, I'd be afraid now that he's dragging me to some separatist group—well, at least there are two other cars in front of the door—or that my last hour has come and my bleached bones just might be found in twenty years, if ever. Pierre confidently pushes open the old door, whose green paint has almost flaked off.

Miraculously, another world opens up. The building, seemingly abandoned to decay, shows its true face: an inn, lit up and furnished. Admittedly, it has somewhat old-fashioned furnishings, but that's exactly what a really good French meal promises. "Mon ami, comment allez-vous?" Kiss left, kiss right, kiss left, on the cheeks of Madame Duran, the restaurant owner, who's getting on a bit in years. But just what does "restaurant" mean here? There was no signpost en route, no sign outside. And, afterwards, on the bill, no imprint, no name. A gourmet joint in disguise—as if it were illegal in France to cook and serve food to guests. But the French love refined cuisine—and simple "bookkeeping." To calculate what sales tax is charged at the counter for wine or liquor at the tables—it's just too complicated for them. Besides, Madame Duran has no time for that. Her husband, who usually helps her, is sick at the moment. Hence, the "simplified" bookkeeping: none at all. That's why, Madame explains, there's only a "streamlined" menu, namely, none at all. She can only make a "salade" with a pâté, Pierre translates. But that sure packed a punch. I've never eaten liver that was so tender. Dessert? Bien sûr, that can't be skipped. Crème brûlée at its best. And then, at some point, Madame Duran comes to our table. In her right hand a bottle of Armagnac, which Pierre fixes with shining eyes, in her left three small glasses. Like a man dying of thirst who has just come from the desert, he stares at the bottle as Madame Duran opens it, and then she pours a golden-yellow, almost brownish content into the small glasses. Pierre can hardly wait — I cast a glance at the old label and try to estimate the price. 120 euros, 200 euros, maybe more. Hopefully, she will at least deduct the sales tax she has saved with her concealed shed.

I don't have a chance to fine-tune my rough thoughts and come up with the crazy idea of calculating the tax — I *could* contemplate such a thing, especially during a wine tasting at the Wirs winery, where after twelve samples I was no longer able to decide which wine to purchase and take home. Pierre had the presence of mind to compensate for my lack of decision-making ability and told Monsieur Wirs: "All of them." I had to gasp a bit at the price, but I didn't object. In France, you don't talk about money, you just spend it like there's no tomorrow. So, Pierre is now hitting me on my shoulder, so hard that I just about spit out my sixth glass of Armagnac. "C'est mon ami Didier d'Allemagne!" he trumpets. "Welcome," says Madame Duran, and wants to know where I'm from. Ah, from "Bonn"—which sounds like "bon." She likes that, a city in Germany with a French name, and such a fun one. For that, she has to top off our glasses right away. "It's bon too, right?" At this, Madame Duran raises the Armagnac bottle triumphantly in the air as if it were a sporting trophy. "Yes, very." I lift my glass triumphantly as well, emptying it. Reflexively, Madame refills it. Then the bottle is empty and I'm glad Pierre wants to go home and doesn't order yet another one. Madame writes ninety euros in her invoice pad. Not as much as I thought. But then, there's no sales tax on it.

3.7 Curiosity

Besides a random double genetic mutation and our almost limitless sexual appetite, developed by our ancestors, and in addition to the presumably even more limitless willingness of males to selflessly disseminate their genetic material, curiosity is an essential motor of human development. Granted, without curiosity we would have reproduced incredibly well, survived all kinds of natural disasters and epidemics, and continued to develop according to the principle of natural selection; we would have become more resilient. But we would never have developed a consciousness with the ability not only to think about problems but also to reflect on our actions.

But I don't intend to go further into that here (even if it would be worthwhile to think about the consequences of one's own curiosity before, for example, building a nuclear bomb). What I would like to point out is that curiosity is a universal phenomenon independent of culture and age, and, most notably, a never-ending flow of human joy, contentment, and gratification. Though this actually requires no further discussion, it's unfortunately often forgotten or neglected.

Yet it's a very inexpensive way to give oneself joy.

4. Active engagement

4.1 Postponement

On the charm of properly procrastinating

"Never put off until tomorrow what you can put off until the day after tomorrow." A waggish utterance from the great Mark Twain. He means, of course, the unpleasant things in life—those we generally like to procrastinate on. Who would exhort others not to let pleasurable things slide? I would, actually. "When will you go to the theater again? You can't keep putting it off." "Treat yourself to something. Don't keep putting it off until tomorrow." You might expect to hear that in advertising, though what they actually mean is: "Indulge us for a change and send us your money."

By encouraging postponement, I of course risk being dragged onto the moral scaffold of psychotherapy by my colleagues. But that doesn't matter; I've been there before.
And there's worse to come. I'm going to speak out both for and against procrastination at the same time. For postponing unpleasant, externally imposed, useless but obligatory things, such as tax returns, weeding, doing your annual accounts, sorting receipts for taxes, writing Christmas cards or postcards when on vacation, obligatory visits to unloved relatives (unless for the pepper harvest, because they've chosen to move to a country that grows this spice), cleaning out the cellar, cleaning the roof tiles, and so on—in short, all the unbearable stuff. But procrastination is only meant as a stopover on the way to eradication. Nonsensical things you're not forced to do should be eliminated. Don't put

them off, but rather get rid of them altogether. That creates time and new energy.

I'm going to speak out for important, fun, unique, personality-enhancing matters and encourage you not to put them off.

Do you remember what you wanted to do when you were sixteen or eighteen? I mean the crazy ideas, projects that were not straightforward, things that were fun and exciting. Things that were more exciting and more conducive to your development than completing a bachelor's degree in business administration in Maastricht — the private university in the Netherlands that has no minimum grade point average to gain admission. I will come back to the "Maastricht topic" later. For now, let's address cycling through Africa, work and travel in Australia, and volunteering in Alaska or Zimbabwe. Many years ago, I met a couple who, aged twenty-three and twenty respectively, did the following: He was a promising computer scientist, she was studying art history, I believe. At that time, computers were as big as wardrobes and art historians still had a chance of getting a job. The computer scientist's sister was marrying a Japanese man and invited the two of them to the wedding. Since there were no low-cost airlines back then, the flights were extremely expensive. As expensive as a good motorbike. "Then let's just travel there by motorbike" — that was his crazy idea. As a rather technically oriented person, he wasn't yet familiar with the detours of the unconscious. He probably didn't even know they existed. So, he took out a map and a calculator. (For the younger generation: Calculators were one-app mobile devices with a number keypad and a minimalist screen.) He estimated the distance, calculated the duration of the journey, and assessed the travel budget. I think he took two months' leave for the round trip and one week at his sister's place. At that time, the two of them didn't yet know that Afghan "highways" were very different from German ones, and that forty kilometers a day was a good average. And that gas was often not available from Aral—a German subsidiary of BP—but only "orally," based on relationships that first had to be established. Otherwise, literally nothing would work. To make a long story short: It took three months for them to reach India. The unconscious is alive in India, and it pulls you in—the two of them spent about half a year there. They visited gurus. And, though it was forbidden, Tibet as well.

I know all too well the feeling of getting pulled in by India. Everything there is calmer, more leisurely. Once, when I visited my friend Sudhir there (he's also a psychoanalyst and writer, but he writes much more important books, and does so better than I do), I saw a construction crew preparing a road for asphalting during road work, which in India is mostly done by hand. It looked more like pantomime, not like efficient work. But that was not what caught my attention. One of the workers was lying motionless in the ditch. Concerned about the man, I approached the worker whom I'd identified as the site manager, given his obvious inactivity. I wanted to know what was wrong with the man. "He's asleep," was his succinct reply. He must have seen from my astonished face what I was wondering in my Western compulsiveness. Before I could even think the sentence, let alone utter it, the site manager replied, "What else is he supposed to do when he's tired?" Taken aback, I had to admit he was right. The site manager shook his head as if to express *how could people ask such stupid questions*. This scene will always remain in my memory.

Yes, that's India. The two learned something important there and decided to act accordingly: In the future, no longer would it be the calendar, but rather their feeling, that would decide how long they would stay in a certain place and when it was time to leave. And crazier and crazier things started to happen. Suddenly, it was no longer a problem to make contact with locals. Even in China, which they were visiting illegally, Chinese people helped the two and gave the runaround to the police, who were always hot on their heels. They did not abandon the plan to congratulate their sister and brother-in-law in Japan, but they did adapt it. In the end, they travelled through Asia and, because it was practically on their way, to Australia. They reached Japan with a small delay of three years. En route, they'd spent their money but also lost their fear. For they had (wisely) decided not to accept money from anyone. Only the motorbikes were repaired free of charge. A matter of honor for the local motorbike workshops or grease monkeys. A note "from the crazy Germans" for the shop wall was enough. They had decided to earn their own living and travel expenses, so they accepted any job, be it in a rice field for a few cents a day, for many yen as German teachers in Japan, or in construction. Then they headed home from Japan via South America, where they crossed the Amazon on a raft they'd built themselves, powered by the motorbikes. On the Pan-American Highway to Alaska, they rode horses; they lived with indigenous people in South America. Then it struck them that they'd completely forgotten one continent: Africa. They explored that too. Then they actually returned to Cologne, on a boat they'd built in South America. In Rotterdam, the Dutch didn't know what to do with the vessel, and they let them sail on to Cologne. The local water police had considerable doubts about the boat's safety; evidently, the pair didn't have a captain's license either. It was no tragedy when the boat was confiscated. After all, they were home again. After sixteen years. In the meantime, the two had become millionaires by chance: After *National Geographic* published a report on them, they were invited to give lectures everywhere, including in Germany. After a year, they'd had enough of Germany and bought a finca in Chile.

Intriguing story. And I've never again met people so free of fear. What's important: The unconscious took them there. There's no career or study counselling that would take you there.

But what's the "normal" fate, the straightforward fate of such dreams? Right: they're postponed. After graduating from high school or college would be the best time. Better get your professional training first. At least a bachelor's degree. But interrupting now? That wouldn't be good either, so just after a master's degree. But what kind of impression does that make on your resume? (I'll get to that in a moment.) So then, look for a job. Learn the ropes, have your contract extended, a contract for an indefinite period, relationship, children, building a house. Oh dear, so it'll be when I retire. That's not a good plan.

What, then, about the argument that a gap in your resume could be your "undoing"? I'll be brief: This is utter nonsense. The opposite is true. Put yourself in the shoes of an employer. You have two young people in front of you, both of whom meet your requirements. One attended college directly after graduating from high school; the other travelled through Africa by bicycle for a year. Who gets your (undivided) attention? At their interviews, what will you ask the one with the straightforward path, and what will you want to find out from the adventurer? Wouldn't you think: Man, oh, man! She's got guts! And stamina — she doesn't give up so easily. She'll certainly be able to deal well with different people. And, hand on heart, who's likely to tell better stories in the cafeteria? If a company psychologist is attending as well, he will presumably attest to her more mature personality.

4.2 Career choice

Choosing the right profession: Why you should never choose a profession without first harvesting melons

The choice of career is one of the only two important decisions in life that can determine lasting contentment or lasting unhappiness. The other decision is choosing the right form of partnership and the right partner. I have already related this to some extent and will return to it.

Everyone will agree that choosing one's professional path is very important. However, priorities are usually set differently. For the majority, particularly the majority of parents, economic security is the decisive criterion. In other words, choosing one's profession such that one has good opportunities in the future and that economic changes or imponderable factors nevertheless offer good — most importantly economically good — prerequisites in order to be able to pursue one's life plan (which I will take a closer look at later). Following this thinking, many end up studying business administration or law because you can "always do something with it."

From a psychological point of view, that's complete nonsense, because if I don't do something with my heart (i.e., full of inner conviction), if I do it without heart and soul, without passion, nothing can come of it. Of course, there are economically successful lawyers or businesspeople — but what I mean here is psychological success, namely, how personally satisfied an economically successful lawyer is.

Does he like going to work? Does she look forward to her clients—or only to her salary or the attorney's fee? Or, at some point, do the boring divorces with the usual bickering, the traffic accidents, and the branches falling from the neighbor's property get on his nerves? In that case, he's heading for burnout. If, on the other hand, he's bored with the cases, if he finds them all similar, he's heading for bore-out. This phenomenon has been known for more than thirty years, but many people, even my colleagues, don't know about it or simply ignore it. The insidious thing about bore-out is that it produces the same symptoms as burnout: physical and mental exhaustion, listlessness, disinterest, sleep disorders, psychosomatic disorders, self-esteem problems, depression, anxiety. If a bore-out is wrongly diagnosed and treated as burnout, then the person affected is "relieved of work," spared. The result is clear: being increasingly under-challenged with more severe symptoms. If the person is sent for treatment to a psychotherapeutic rehabilitation facility and is spared even more there, his situation will deteriorate further. In the worst case, he will be advised to retrain for a job that will take even more strain off him.

> "Choose a job you love, and you will never work a day in your life."

The sage Confucius is supposed to have said that. I can tell you from my own experience that it's true. A person who enjoys her work does not already fret on Sunday evening that she'll have to return to her unloved activity on Monday. She looks forward to her work.

"Isn't it a difficult path to get there? Isn't it impossible to achieve?" some may ask. I can say no—if you've given yourself time to "feel" what is right for you. You should forget statistics, because destinies are not written by statistics. Nor are they written by calculating probabilities. Most people distrust such calculations anyway. How else can one explain that every Saturday about one out of every four Germans heads to a lottery kiosk, even though the probability of winning the main prize of 1.5 million euros is 1:14 million. That is, close to nil—about 150 out of 20 million players get it every year. And 40 percent tax is deducted from the stakes before they go into the lottery drawing. Author Kurt Tucholsky once called this a tax on dumb people. If I were to tell you that, according to a scientific study by the University of Cologne, winnings last an average of four years ... but I won't.

Imagine you show up at the lottery kiosk on a Saturday morning, intending maybe just to buy a newspaper to read yesterday's news, and the cashier asks you: "Would you like to give four euros to the state? And spring for six euros for others for a gamble where you have next to no chance of winning anything? And if you do win, the money will be gone after four years. You won't get your job back either, the one you quit despite your good intentions. Nor will you be eligible for unemployment benefits." I'm sure the lottery kiosk would close down soon after that. Nevertheless, twenty million Germans head there every year, voluntarily paying extra taxes. This, despite the popular sport (presumably not only among Germans), to cheat on one's taxes wherever possible. My tip to the finance minister: Increase the main prize to ten million, and tax lottery income at 90 percent. You think that doesn't work out statistically? Oh, yes it does, quite easily: instead of six out of forty-nine, you decrease the odds to six out of fifty-nine! I assure you, no lottery player will do the math! You could also advertise that such a win lasts for 40 years. It's not true, of course. I'd guess it's more like six. But we needn't tell anyone that.

Why shouldn't this also apply to the choice of profession? Quite simply: because we have no influence on the choice of lottery numbers. You can fill out your forms with as much commitment and heart as you can muster and watch the Lotto Fairy on TV as passionately as you'd like; it won't help. The lotto numbers are just ping-pong balls with forty-nine numbers written on them. And they're drawn by a machine, not selected. The ping-pong balls have no plan, no will, nothing. The number combinations are random. The probability that next Saturday the same combination of numbers will come up as the last draw is the same as it is for any other combination. But it's more likely another one will come up, because there are about 14 million other combinations. You don't believe me? I have a confession to make: I was once in a casino. Not in Monaco, but in Saint-Raphaël. At a single table, the number one came up seven times within a quarter of an hour. I went ahead and sat down and after another quarter of an hour my two hundred euros were gone—the number one simply did not appear again. I learned the hard way. Too bad, I should have treated myself to a good Armagnac instead. That, too, would be gone today, but I'd have a better memory!

We can indeed influence our professional path and our career. Before you get nervous: I'm not one of those trickster coaches who speak in packed civic centers and leave with a bulging bank account, having fooled thousands into thinking they can be successful. "If you only want to. If you approach things full of energy and without any doubts!" That's not just nonsense; firing people up like that is even dangerous and, in my opinion, should be banned.

What I mean is a choice made with passion and heart, finding something that corresponds to your own self, the needs of your unconscious, your personality. In short: things that you like to do, that you do voluntarily, that you have fun with, that you're curious about. But before that, another question is important:

Do I want only to earn money with my profession —
or do I also want self-actualization?

Many would probably spontaneously say: both, of course. That's understandable, but the following considerations are worth thinking about.

There can be benefits to only wanting to earn money with my work and to then use that money to indulge my passions in my free time. These needn't always be mundane pleasures like sport or travel. I can also express myself artistically (only 1 percent of freelance artists in Germany can make a living from their art alone) or engage myself socially, as Albert Schweitzer did, for example. He was a doctor and organist, but he didn't want to become rich. Instead, he had a dream of founding a hospital in Gabon. For everyone, not just for the well-off! Since he could earn more money in

Europe with organ concerts, he did so — and took the money to Africa.

If you are not so good at playing the organ, you could also start an internet business to avoid taking up vocational training. Or do the training to have a secure income and maybe even end up in an office. What is important for your satisfaction balance is that you have something you are passionate about. And that the job or the work you do without passion and lifeblood demands only so much of you that you have enough strength and desire in your leisure time to pursue what actually makes your heart beat faster. If you are exhausted, annoyed, or frustrated in the evening, you'll probably soon lose the desire for it. You should keep this in mind when choosing your work on a purely financial basis. In this context, it also seems important to ask whether you run the risk of becoming bored with the job one day. As already described, this has a frustrating and toxic effect.

This can be remedied by a certain flexibility option built in from the start, namely if your choice of profession opens you up to many areas of activity. For example, if you work in event management, helping with planning or set-up, you can switch to another provider. Those who become civil servants out of fear of unemployment get a "life sentence" — and they get it without parole, in contrast to criminals, who can be released after fifteen years. Those who seek security externally often have no security internally and have a great fear of breaking out of the cage they have built for themselves. The two world travelers showed that real (i.e., lasting) security can only be found within one's own self.

This way of earning money has an enormous advantage. Although you tend to have to do without security, you gain a maximum of freedom—including external freedom. You are more open to coincidences in life, which you are more likely to encounter in this configuration than in the secure domain. I once met a person (he would prefer to remain anonymous) who related the following incident to me. He was a lawyer and got to know a young man on the golf course. This man cheekily asked him whether he would like to invest ten thousand dollars in his business, as he was looking for another business partner. The lawyer found the idea the young man presented to him quite bizarre, absurd, and even dangerous. Who, after all, would want to buy books on the internet? Everyone knew the best place to buy books was a bookstore. Even the name of the company, which the young man intended to take from a Latin American river, showed the lawyer that the guy had to be a megalomaniac and a crackpot. He clearly wanted the money to build a home in cloud cuckoo land. The lawyer didn't want to tell me what he did with the ten thousand dollars he saved.

Such encounters needn't always take place on the golf course, nor do they have to be of this dimension; but they're unlikely to happen if you're a civil servant sitting around in a clerk's office. And if they do, you won't have the freedom and courage to seize the opportunity. Of course, it's always good to be careful and not to place one's money, energy and chances in life on the line unnecessarily, as in a lottery.

I can tell you one thing: The lawyer can look in the mirror in the morning knowing that he, for one, pays his employees fairly.

I once became a journalist through a chance meeting. (I've always had several professions at the same time—pursuing just one was too limiting for me). A friend was offered a job as a freelance local reporter, but he wasn't interested. I was eighteen, had just finished school, and had no specific career path in mind yet. To pick up on Mark Twain's joke, there was no honest work to be had at the time. Through other coincidences I ended up first in radio, then in television. At some point I made documentaries (I'd thought about becoming a filmmaker), and in the end I had my own film production company, which I used to finance my studies and my therapeutic training.

Only in rare cases do people who choose the safe way of earning money do so out of conviction—more out of embarrassment, indecision, impatience, panic, or some other internal or external pressure. "Some" profession is chosen. Not deliberately, but also not thoroughly felt (i.e., done without inner conviction).

The pressure young people put on themselves today, and that their parents put on them, is tremendous, and it just keeps growing. Often parents come to me with "Maastricht syndrome," as I've called it, meaning the child is supposed to study in Maastricht (success-oriented parents seem to lose their bearings and end up with me); that's how he or she will have the best chances later. But the deadline for applications is approaching fast, and he or she (usually he) doesn't want to apply. The ink on the high school diploma is not quite dry yet, but things are supposed to proceed. A gap must be avoided at all costs, or else he'll have no chances later. Couldn't I talk to him, man to man, the parents ask. I'm supposed to convince him, but, in reality, I'm supposed to manipulate him. Does he actually *want* to study business, I ask? Does he know you're here? What would you think if he came to me and asked me, for example, to persuade you to pay him his inheritance now? What's it really about? His parents are worried because he doesn't know yet what he wants. Maybe he needs therapy? No, he doesn't need therapy, he needs some quiet time to think things through.

But then he would lose a year. How awful to have your bachelor's degree at age twenty-two and your master's at twenty-four. If you plan your life like a trip on an express train, precisely planning all the stops and arrival and departure times, you will probably get to your destination more quickly—and already have burnout at thirty-five, which gives you time to reorient yourself during this phase of work incapacity and retrain in another profession. Not bad, this planning, but why the diversions? Why not start with orientation? Without burnout, perhaps on a slow train, and including sightseeing tours in cities or even longer stays along the way.

If nothing helps and the situation at home escalates, because often parents just can't let go, I recommend the "melon therapy," as I once called it. One year of work and travel in Australia. The young person is allowed to travel and work as much as they want. Most work for three months and travel for nine, even though the parents might prefer it the other way around. I call it melon therapy because many of these young people work as melon harvesters. Don't worry, these are not those huge Turkish things that look like green aerial bombs and are just as heavy. Even if you might expect otherwise from Australia, the melons there are more the size of honeydew melons. About the size of the young people's eyes when they start to light up as I tell them about this possibility.

Why so far away? There are several reasons. For one thing: You can't get farther away from home. The parents can't just check whether everything's okay; they're forced to let go. But what seems most important to me: The young person also moves far away internally from parental values. He is protected from their panicky nagging, which brings nothing but bad moods and reactance anyway. He can learn to feel (again) and discover new people and other lifestyles. Live with the Aborigines and try out one or two things, even if they're not all legal. That year will take the young person further in his or her personal development than any course of study at an elite university. It is also advisable to go far away so that it becomes a challenge for the young person. He learns to master it, copes with difficult situations, discovers abilities in himself that he didn't know before—or is compelled to develop because he can't just drop by home for a while. This strengthens the young person's self-esteem and character, because he can develop better than under the strict supervision of his mom and dad. They only want the best for him. But that's not how to bring it about, as he is coming to discover for himself now. That's why a country closer by isn't suitable.

Don't worry, so far, no one has come back as a junkie or turned into a permanent Oblomov. The young people have always come back stronger in many ways; they know themselves and life better than before and have become more courageous. And above all: they've come back as originals, not copies of their parents.

We are all originals when we're born. And it means the greatest happiness to remain an original and not become a copy of someone else.

Once we've made this first decision wholeheartedly in favor of "I want to do more than just earn money," the next question is, automatically, what we want to do.

4.3 Success

Why success is important after all — even if that gets misunderstood

Why am I now saying success is, in fact, important? After all, I previously recommended a different path. For this, we have to look at what is commonly understood as success — and what I understand as success, namely, a healthier point of view.

In society — whoever or whatever "society" is — success is primarily evaluated as a person's "overall balance sheet." Meaning, how much she earns today, what job she has, how much profit she makes, what titles she has, and so on. If at age forty-five you're still not a senior doctor, you've "done something wrong" — or so we're led to believe. The same goes for anyone who hasn't built a house yet at thirty-eight. And for someone who is still working on a degree at twenty-eight and is not yet a professor at thirty-two. Anyone who is still tinkering with his old Beetle at age fifty-one rather than driving a "suitable" midsize sedan, likewise. Even if it's not officially said or attested: You are "out," excluded. You are patronized and not taken seriously; in the eyes of others, you're a failure. Yet we live in a culture in which everyone is supposed to be "included"; no one is supposed to be excluded. Officially, it's considered morally reprehensible if people with disabilities, asylum seekers, people of color, homosexuals, Muslims, etc. are excluded. People who are not successful in the social sense don't seem to be included in this category worthy of protection. They can be called failures with impunity. I think this is just as discriminatory, because many circumstances are not taken into account here. For one thing, we cannot choose our genes, nor our basic cognitive equipment, nor our character.

Secondly, we each grow up in different circumstances. We cannot choose whether we are born into a household of professors, or as a child of millionaires, blue-collar workers, or civil servants, or born into a family of drinkers or violent parents.

Thirdly, only to a limited extent can we influence how we are judged by others and whether our personality is recognized and, fourthly, valued, and whether we are supported accordingly. The greatest talent is of little use if it's not recognized. And even if this is the case, it's still governed by the fate of parental appreciation. Thus, an intellectual talent may be seen as pointless in a family of craftspeople, perhaps because the child is supposed to take over her parents' business one day, or for protective reasons, so as not to feel dumber than one's own child. On the other hand, an academic family often cannot bear their child's wish to learn a trade.

Fifthly, there may be possible "attempts at distortion" in hopes of influencing the fate of a person's inclinations and talent. An intellectually talented person in a family of craftspeople could be pushed to study timber construction, because then the family would have a respectable engineer in the company. The same can happen in a family with high educational qualifications, such as if the daughter is persuaded to become a nurse rather than a car mechanic. The parents' secret hope could be: Maybe she'll enjoy medicine and go to university later. And then they would avoid the presumed embarrassment of having to explain to their illustrious circle of like-minded people why their daughter is not interested in an academic career, and whether they may be able to drive that out of her. All the while, the daughter loves the smell of fresh engine oil and is as "happy as a snow queen" whenever she makes a spluttering engine purr.

Sixthly, the right support is just as crucial for the "fate of success." Fatally, it's often gifted children who don't receive sufficient support, because their parents think that, given their cleverness, they'll make it on their own. Some parents also don't know how to support their children; perhaps they're selfish and delegate that responsibility to the school. But schools, too, are usually overextended, and need to recognize the talent in the first place. Many gifted students are classified as less gifted because they disconnect in class when not challenged enough. The danger of bore-outs begins early—right after birth, strictly speaking; parents with babies who thirst for knowledge know what I'm talking about. On the other hand: unfortunately, some parents these days consider their perfectly normal child highly gifted.

I don't intend to list in detail the other possible construction sites, road closures, and detours en route to a fulfilling professional life.

Three other societal misconceptions seem important to me when assessing whether someone is successful. Firstly, the time it took for someone to achieve something, and, secondly, at what age he or she achieved it. There are ostensibly clear scorecards intended to pseudo-objectify the assessment. A ninety-two-year-old (the real-life example can be found on the Internet) working toward a PhD is highly respected, even though it may have taken her longer than others. A forty-year-old who achieves the same after fifteen years at university quickly ends up in the "failure" category. Her summa cum laude is then of little use. Many probably think: That's the least you can expect after all this time. Just as an aside: Do you know how long a dissertation in archeology takes on average? What would you guess? Five years? Six years? No, it's exactly twelve. You've never heard? That's probably because archaeology is an extremely modest science. Though it can celebrate the smallest success as sensational, for example, when the engraving of drinking cups of a Mayan culture, which until now seemed regionally limited, is found five hundred kilometers away, in slightly modified form. Nevertheless, archaeologists tend to remain modest, since such discoveries do not change the world. And they don't want to find Atlantis either, since they know the "big things," should they still exist, are more likely to be found by chance than by obsessive digging. Archeologists also don't dig with a shovel excavator but with a teaspoon and a toothbrush. Even the smallest shards are photographed, documented, and catalogued.

I'll say more about modesty and patience later. But here, I'll say this much: Passion can also be exercised slowly, quietly, and softly.

When we judge—arrogantly, it seems to me—that a person took too long to do something or started too late, we forget to ask why it took longer than usual. There can be good reasons for this. Perhaps they had to finance their education on their own, had children, became ill, cared for their parents or other relatives. Nevertheless, this doesn't suffice to rehabilitate this person and to recognize his or her accomplishment as on a par with others. If, however, this person reveals that he or she preferred to study at a comfortable pace, lived for a year in the caves of Valle Gran Rey, or meditated in the Finca Argayall, none of that will be recognized but rather patronized. He will probably be dismissed as a crackpot. Personally, incidentally, I find weirdos more interesting than middle-class bourgeois people, because I'm interested in what goes on in the hearts and minds of interesting people. But that's another topic with which I've made myself unpopular with many colleagues. Fortunately, not only do I not care about that, but on the contrary: In the end, you need to have the right enemies. More about that later, too.

The next and very weighty, and faulty, measurement of success is money. Money in the form of monthly paychecks or property or other assets—that's the official measure of success. Substitutes can be athletic, literary, or academic success. If money and one of the latter come together, the official evaluation is even better. Nonetheless, the calculation still must withstand being divided by the time it has taken to get there. Those who get rich quickly are at the top. In public opinion, it doesn't matter how someone achieved success. Did they achieve or invent something on their own, or at the expense of others, or even by stealing ideas? Not only does the social responsibility factor not play a role, but it's deliberately swept under the rug.

Few are interested in the fact that Jeff Bezos tries wherever possible to drive down the wages of his employees, without whom he would never have become rich, or to shift distribution centers to neighboring countries, worsening the ecological footprint, or the fact that he puts his profits in tax havens. What matters is that he has two hundred billion dollars. Nobody really wants to know he was one of the people who profited from the COVID-19 pandemic.

Incidentally, I still prefer to order my books locally, at buchLaden 46, a small neighborhood bookshop.

But let's look at an alternative scenario. What if socially recognized success were not measured by how much someone has created, but how he or she has achieved it and for whom? If we didn't ask how long it took him or her, but with what effort, commitment, self-sacrifice, and perseverance they achieved it? And whether they have treated and paid their employees fairly—including those in developing countries? How would it be if we measured success according to how ecologically sustainably a company operates?

Those are the values I would like to see.

In summary: Social norms can exert tremendous pressure to follow the prescribed paths. The fact is very few enjoy living in this cloud-cuckoo land of a prison, not daring to flee only because they are afraid of freedom, perhaps a little too lazy to get off their butts, and possibly also too comfortable to take responsibility—more on this later.

4.4 Self-efficacy

We need self-efficacy more urgently than "tremendous successes"

Our self-esteem is built out of individual experiences that confirm to us in two dimensions that we are effective and our personal existence matters. One dimension is the direct experience of the self-efficacy of one's own actions: I can bring about or achieve something. This can be a little tower a toddler builds or a cake a young confectioner makes that she's satisfied with. In this way, I confirm to myself I can do something. Though these experiences are often called into question by failures, in the long run the results accumulate and become a stable component of our personality. At some point, I no longer have to ask myself whether I can read. I know it, and there's no indication I could lose this quality. So, at some point, we acquire a crystalline part to our self-esteem in contrast to the larger fluid one. This means everything we're not able to do or not yet able to do well enough that we would call it stable. The fluid realm is home to our pride. Even if we are unshakably convinced of our ability, it's good now and again to experience that we have done something well in a certain domain. A goal scorer in soccer would never say: Now that I know I can score goals, I don't need to score any more.

The other dimension is the community. Doing something that benefits another person or group also creates experiences of self-efficacy and thus good self-esteem.

What many don't know, or don't pay attention to, is that when they repress or deny negative self-efficacy experiences (i.e., when we harm others) this also has an effect on our self-esteem balance. Taking the cash out of the wallet you found and claiming to the lost property office that it was empty increases our wealth but damages our self-esteem. The next time you find a wallet, take pleasure in the face of the person who lost it and who marvels that everything is still inside.

I even believe that prosocial behavior is "burned into" our personalities just as much as antisocial behavior. You can somehow sense whether someone is a good person, a nice person — or a scoundrel.

What matters when choosing a career is to ask oneself what kind of activity has, so far, given me the most satisfying self-efficacy experiences.

It is worth reflecting, too, that I may be doing the job for forty or fifty years or even longer. Is that okay with me, or will I eventually be bored by it? Or annoyed because, at some point, when the activity has become routine, it may also get on my nerves?

If you answer yes to the last question, or if you're not sure whether a clear no would be appropriate, you should ask yourself whether this activity offers possibilities for variation. As a carpenter, could I perhaps also work in shipbuilding? Could I become self-employed? Go into development work? Teach at a vocational school? What's important is that I can maintain what I value about the profession, what I enjoy.

But the most important thing remains: You should not pursue a profession without heart and soul and passion. (And ideally not pursue other things without those factors either.) Unfortunately, life, or, rather, our fellow human beings, sometimes like to torture us—I think they really like doing it—with boring, nonsensical, stupid jobs.

To do something, we need either our own motivation, (i.e., a drive) or pressure from outside. In short: Either with utter conviction and determination or with a gun put to your head—how would you prefer to work? Well, I'd rather be dragged away from my desk than dragged to it.

4.5 Heart and passion

Can you be successful without heart and soul and passion? Even if the conclusion seems obvious after the preceding chapters, I don't want to answer the question with a clear "no." Maybe with some jobs, the fun part comes only after a certain time. Possibly when counting money. But I would like to urge caution: We humans possess strong self-deception mechanisms. With their help, we can survive imprisonment in camps or other tough situations. This is a sensible mechanism provided by evolution. Unfortunately, evolution couldn't keep up with our development—we have long since overtaken it. Homo erectus became Homo connectus, searching no longer for food but for Wi-Fi.

And so, we can delude ourselves into thinking the smartphone is a useful, indispensable helper without which we would not get through everyday life. We ignore the fact that we often solve problems with our smartphone we wouldn't even have without it.

But let's return to the initial question. Imagine the following: There's an apprenticeship as a motorcycle mechanic in your area. Not only is it well-paid (you've never had so much money in your pocket), but it's also just ten minutes from your parents' house. But you don't give a hoot about motorbikes, and you'd rather become a pastry chef. For that job, however, you'd have to get up half an hour earlier and you'd have a hundred euros less in your pocket. What's more, motorcyclists get on your nerves. Let's further assume that you make it through the motorbike mechanic apprenticeship, perhaps you even agonize your way to getting a master craftsperson's title, and ultimately you open a motorbike workshop. Your master craftsperson's certificate hangs on the wall, certifying that you passed the exam with flying colors and you are allowed to practice this profession.

Everything is in place: lifting platforms, a compressed air system, toolboxes. The only thing missing is your enthusiasm, the gleam in your eyes when a customer shows up with a Horex Imperator, built in 1955. A real aficionado would immediately have to inspect it from all angles and then pat the proud owner on the back because he simply can't help it and say: "Man, this is really in good shape, everything is still original! How did you manage that?" "Yes, well I picked it up four years ago in a shed in Saarland — you wouldn't believe what it looked like — here are a few photos. Three years of work. But now she's something to behold." "Kudos, you've done a great job. I don't know whether I could have done it that well." "Yes, that's my baby." I bet the place would then be "humming." Maybe it would even attain cult status among bikers. Incidentally, the friends William S. Harley and Arthur Davidson were just as passionate at the beginning of the 20th century — I think you know the product.

But if you ask the same customer, who appears at your doorway just before closing time, a bit grumpily what you can do for him (you actually mean what can he do for you) — do you really think you would be just as successful? And more importantly: How satisfied would you be with yourself?

A true aficionado will probably be happy to extend his working day by half an hour, and, when he gets home, he'll tell his partner, who, "wisely" is also enthusiastic about motorcycles (hers is a 1976 Yamaha single cylinder): "Sorry, darling, that I'm late, but you won't believe it: a guy came in earlier who'd patched together an original Horex Imperator himself, one built in 1955. I put a new cylinder head gasket on it." "What, really, they still exist? Why didn't you call me?" Okay, maybe that's a bit of an exaggeration—such partnerships are probably even rarer than a 1955 Horex Imperator.

Many parents push their children onto professional paths and into studying subjects that the children themselves reject deep inside. Perhaps they choose them anyway because they are tired of their parents' nagging, because nothing better to do occurs to them, or because they've panicked, they've been driven into doing so.

Law and business management are the classics. These people often show up in my psychotherapy practice because they've developed a learning disorder. This develops because they've been deluding themselves for too long that their studies would be fun. Yet, after just one semester, it's become clear to them the subject is boring, the lecturers uptight and demanding, and their fellow students are dull. It's not their world. Now they're afraid, even panicking, that there'll be nothing else for them in life. I always try to bring East Frisian calmness to the matter—modelled on the relaxed mindset I encounter in that part of coastal northern Germany. Because often young people want to study something else right away. "But what should I choose? Can you tell me?" *Mu*, the Zen Buddhist would say, to all questions to which there are no answers.

If you don't have a destination, no matter how fast you travel, you will never arrive.

You can quote me if you like. Just be sure to properly attribute the quote, or I'll get mad.

As to the person mentioned above, they will have to feel their way to the answer. That takes time. They know that in East Frisia.

4.6 Chaos

The charm of chaos

"Nothing can exist without order. Nothing new can emerge without chaos." Albert Einstein said.

Order is a fine thing; good old Goethe already knew that. He kept his houses meticulously tidy — with the exception of his writing rooms, where creative chaos reigned. Yet he left great works and inventions to posterity. Few people know he invented modern speech-to-text conversion (i.e., Siri and Alexa) at the time, without wires and without a PC or smartphone. But that's another story. Order is a nice thing; tidying up, on the other hand, isn't. Tidying up is an infinitely uncreative and unpleasant task. I don't think there's anyone who, when asked whether she has time on the weekend, would answer: "No, I don't, I'm going to tidy up. I'm so looking forward to it." More like: "I have to tidy up on the weekend. But what can you offer as an excuse?"

Still, order is considered an important virtue. But ask yourself where it's really important, and where it's executed against your will as a distorted compulsion to fulfil some norm we don't know or don't understand or, in any case, don't accept. A friend of mine (she prefers not to be named) has her own form of order. Namely, none. When you visit her and she asks you whether you'd like a cup of tea, she mosaically pushes things aside to make space on the coffee table, separating the sea of things stored there so that precisely one cup fits among it all. Then she disappears into the kitchen, and it's easy to tell from the clattering noises that she's looking for cups in the sink and rinsing them off. On her desk, there's a layer of papers at least twenty centimeters high. Fortunately, she's a paper geologist: she knows exactly the chronology of the documents, and so she knows at what height a letter can be found from March—from the year before last, of course. But she always has time, and she's always in a good mood.

Residents of Provence and the Côte d'Azur take a similarly relaxed view. Those who have a house usually also have a shed. Everything that gets in the way in the house goes in there. Clean it out? Far from it. "And what happens when the shed is full?" I once asked. "Then we build a new one." That works too. You'll probably never see anyone painting shutters in the south of France either, but you will see shutters with faded paint, sometimes hanging on by a single hinge. And what happens if that breaks? Then the shutters are placed under the window. Or in the shed. I will have more to tell you about France in the next chapter.

My private documents are not neatly filed in neatly labeled folders, as would be the typical German style, but are instead stashed in two boxes. I label one with the current year; the other one is for insurance-related stuff. After two years have passed, I throw away old years without giving them another look, and, while I'm at it, I clean out the insurance box. My friend Sudhir in India has "natural helpers" who dispose of the old files in accordance with data protection regulations: termites. They eat everything, down to the last page. Unfortunately, importing Indian termites is prohibited in Germany.

4.7 Time and money

Time killers and pleasure killers

Time now for a few reflections on time. In France, time often stands still for me. That's due not only to Pierre, but also to the pastis, and to the quintessential French slowness. Incidentally, the French also don't waste any time in disentangling the bills in restaurants. While many groups in Germany struggle with dividing up in a complicated way who had which drinks, and in doing so torture and confuse the waiter—they recalculate at least three times, and, in the end, there's always one beer left over, so the whole thing starts all over again; you could say the waiter doesn't get a tip, but damages for pain and suffering—it's easier in France: 92.50 euros, four friends, four wallets, four times 25 euros, fits perfectly! What counts is the amusement.

If I answered every email with a personal note ("Thank you for your enquiry, blah blah, and so on, and so forth"), I wouldn't get anywhere. I get at least a hundred emails a day, usually about two hundred. That would also be a great preparation course for hell, which in my imagination is digital, by the way—filled with computers that don't work. Or maybe that would be heaven? No idea. In any case, I have neither the time nor the inclination. "Is the meeting tomorrow at 3 p.m.?" Answer: "Yes." Rude? No. And that's what led me to invent my "20-second rule," which, if I may say so myself, I think is ingenious. It goes like this: Anything that comes in, in terms of new tasks or new tortures, I check to see whether I can do it in twenty seconds. A "French 20 seconds," meaning, roughly, what feels like twenty seconds—like the above-mentioned email. Open it, type three letters into the keyboard, and it's gone.

Things that can't be completed in twenty seconds, because I would need to be angry about the thing for five minutes or cuss for ten minutes, are divided into the following categories: unimportant, important, very important, particularly important, and truly important. And then I "work my way through" them. Meaning I consider—very briefly, of course—whether I'll postpone the emails or tasks until tomorrow, the day after tomorrow, next week, or next year. It's usually not quite that bad; most people get an answer quickly: within three months. More urgent things should be requested from me by letter.

In the process, I've made a rather important discovery: It's not just eggplant or fish that have an expiration date, emails do too. Letters as well. And after a while, a lot of things have already taken care of themselves. Who would have thought? Me, of course!

Why do you always have to answer an email or a text message immediately?

Most people would say: because it's expected. Imagine the mail carrier were to come, ring your doorbell, hand you a letter, and expect you to read the letter immediately and send the answer back with him. Pretty absurd, right? That's exactly how those who send emails or text messages behave. But you don't have to go along with every bit of nonsense.

It's only the pastis that must come tout de suite—immediately.

5. Responsibility and self-care

5.1 Authentic

Being authentic:
why you shouldn't contort or deny yourself

This chapter is particularly close to my heart. We are born as originals, and we shouldn't turn ourselves into copies. At first, we are expected to make great efforts to adapt, a process also called socialization, or upbringing, which for me smacks of manipulation with the aim of suppressing naturalness. The argument is that this adaptation is necessary for others. One could object that a certain "education" or "upbringing" really is necessary, especially to curb selfish motives that harm other people, the community at large, or the environment. The environmental aspect is still quite a new one. Even one hundred years ago, no one was thinking about how sensitive the ecological balance is. Yet one needs to take into account that people have only known about the consequences for some fifty years. Today, no one can say anymore that they didn't know. Respect for other peoples or ethnic groups is also relatively new. The colonial era was not so long ago—into the fifties of the twentieth century it seemed a matter of course to exploit and enslave some peoples, who were often designated as "savages." Today, many in the Global North want to send the "economic refugees" away rather than take responsibility for the consequences.

We humans live in a constant discrepancy between needs that benefit ourselves and needs that benefit the community. If my own needs—I'll call them self-referring needs here—do not harm others or the community, there's no conflict.

Let's imagine a researcher who for egotistical reasons (and who can be free of them) is searching for a cure for a disease hitherto deemed incurable. Perhaps she is secretly aiming for the Nobel Prize, a professorship, or greater recognition. Or she wants to patent her medicine to become rich. Since she ultimately benefits others by being in the laboratory all the time, no one will hold it against her — except perhaps her family. If, in contrast, she works in a laboratory where crystal meth is produced, it's probably a different case.

The crucial question, in my view, is whether we humans can, by nature, muster enough compassion for others to take responsibility for our behavior, such that we don't need any instruction but only a few small corrections here and there.

I think we can, and that we have that capacity by nature. Why am I so sure about this? Because otherwise we wouldn't exist. Only our community spirit and the desire not to harm others has helped us to survive.

Why is that? I believe it lies in our desire for attachment and relationships to others. We develop this ability as infants. While the infant initially seems to be a ruthless new fellow human being, the prototype of an egoist who seems quite indifferent to other people's needs, and for whom considerateness is an alien concept, from about the fifth month onwards he or she develops behavior exhibiting elements of guilt and fear, leading to a reduction in demanding reactions. Melanie Klein called this the "depressive position."

At first, the primary force is the infant's fear of losing the mother as an "object" necessary for survival. Later, we recognize the other qualities of closeness in relationships and don't want to do without them. Not only because we experience them as beautiful and pleasant, but because we humans need this closeness.

In any case, the actual "correction" of antisocial behavior, cited by so many educators as a necessity for social behavior, takes place in the social context.

Along with the importance of relationships for us humans and our attachment needs, we develop empathy from around the age of four. We can put ourselves in others' shoes and feel as they do, even if we may not be in the same (emergency) situation at that moment. And, because we care about others, we will stop ourselves in many actions—and we learn to ask permission. "May I snuggle up with you?" for example.

Of course, there are also actions we at first do not know could harm others. Or we weren't able to think about the consequences of our actions beforehand—for example, if our grandmother's favorite cup falls on the floor. It remains the case, however, that people are more likely to be willing to help than to want to harm others.

Although this is anchored in our genetic disposition, it can also be steered in the wrong direction if we don't have the following experiences. On the one hand, we need an environment (i.e., parents), a family in which we are welcome and can feel that. We need loving parents to experience ourselves as lovable people and our environment as loving and not harmful. We then speak of the "internalization of a good object." This refers to a certain inner conviction and positive, humane attitude that enables us to treat ourselves and others well. An egotistical conflict of "I *or* the other person" becomes "I *and* the other person" or "I *and* you."

The second factor that either fosters this positive development or affects it negatively is observational learning. I hardly need to explain this. Parents who preach compassion but do not model it will only produce new lying preachers. That's because we don't learn through language, but from examples.

Later, empathy is joined by identification. We like the other person so much that we want to be like them. Or we identify with the community and its goals, so that we go to a Fridays for Future demonstration or join a protest against clearcutting a forest. There are two different forms of identification here: with the ethical values and with the group itself.

Nevertheless, selfishness and inconsiderateness exist — whether these are increasing, as many believe, I cannot say. At all times in human existence there have been individuals who have behaved inconsiderately (i.e., to the detriment of others). Times when there are no fixed communities that would note and disapprove of this behavior of course make it easier for such people. This observation displeases us to some extent as a form of social control, exercised ostensibly to protect the common good but benefitting only a few privileged individuals. Examples may be seen in the guild system, which was intended to achieve control over the market under the guise of quality assurance (a kind of medieval consumer protection) or, in modern times, when tax reforms ostensibly benefit hard-working people, but in reality are intended to flatten progression. You didn't understand the latter? That's good, because that's the intention. If you understood the truth behind it, namely, that the top taxation rate is being lowered at the same time, you would probably be rather annoyed.

If you knew the top taxation rate in Germany is 46.5 percent, you would also wonder how that could be possible. So, in plain language: if a person has one hundred million euros in pre-tax profits—that means revenue minus operating expenses, minus money shifted to subsidiaries, minus money shifted to other foreign companies, minus money shifted to foundations (surely there are other possibilities to reduce the taxable amount, but the malicious portions of my imagination are not sufficient)—that person pays 46.5 million euros in taxes on it. And we can already hear those affected complaining loudly because they don't see that they have 53.5 million left. 53.5 million to spend, meaning 4.45 million per month. Or 146,000 euros per day. I think most readers would be happy if they earned half that net per year, or do you earn more than 6,700 euros net per month? That's why I am convinced that 6,000 euros is enough.

5.2 Courage

Why courage is healthy and important

From 1981 onwards, people gathered in St. Nicholas Church in the East German city of Leipzig for peace prayers, with which they wanted to express their hope for an improvement of the inhuman situation in the German Democratic Republic. After eight years, on September 4, 1989, a thousand of them plucked up their courage and initiated a forbidden demonstration through the streets of Leipzig. Since they could not see into the future, this was a very risky action that could have ended in beatings, death, or years of bullying in prison. A thousand out of 16.7 million people, clearly a minority—superficially, at least. One month later there were already twenty thousand people protesting in the streets, and two months later three hundred thousand people participated. They brought the ailing system crashing down. Probably no one expected on September 4, 1989, that almost exactly two months later they would topple the Berlin Wall.

The development of our species has been predominantly influenced, promoted, and pushed by courageous and nonconformist people. Unfortunately, it must be admitted, not always for the best, as we are now experiencing with the consequences of climate change. But even in the "heyday" of our capitalist megalomania, there were cautionary voices warning about the consequences or against the dangers of nuclear power. Nevertheless, much of what courageous people have achieved has been for the benefit of humankind.

On December 1, 1955, Rosa Parks, a 42-year-old seamstress, was travelling on a public bus to her job in Montgomery, Alabama. Another passenger boarded the bus and demanded Parks vacate her seat immediately. Was Parks sitting in a seat reserved for passengers with physical disabilities? No. She was Black, he was white. Rosa Parks was seated in the "Black" section but was asked to stand when the seats "reserved" for whites filled up—an arrogance that seems incredible today. Her arrest and conviction led to the 13-month Montgomery bus boycott, which ended with the U.S. Supreme Court ruling that segregation on public transport systems is unconstitutional.

Courageous people live by their own inner rules. Rosa Parks simply and clearly said "no." She hardly anticipated what would happen as a result.

5.3 Caring and self-care

I have already written a lot about the important function of the care we receive from others or give to them. Equally important, however, is self-care: Only if we consider ourselves to be beings worthy of love and protection do we watch our personal boundaries and our health.

As a psychotherapist, I have to do this all the time for professional reasons. There are three conditions for self-care. Firstly, I must consider myself important and worthy enough that it's natural to protect myself against overexertion, detriments to health, illnesses, or overstrain. Secondly, I need to sharpen my self-awareness in this area. I deliberately do not write "develop" it, because we humans have mastered this since birth. As infants, we fight back when we find something unpleasant or feel overloaded or overwhelmed. If we are exposed to too many stimuli that overtax our natural stimulus-response barrier, we first begin to whine and then cry if there's no reaction. Only over the course of our lives do we disavow the stimuli from the unconscious that signals us to leave a situation or stop an activity. We are asked, against our convictions, to be patient, to persevere, to endure unpleasant things, or take up activities abhorrent to us. This is a double-edged sword because a few things are mixed up here, in my opinion, that have nothing to do with each other. On the one hand, humans are the only living beings that have managed to develop drive mechanisms beyond what is actually necessary. Every living being has a biological program that controls, for example, the intake of food. No field hamster would clear the entire maize field in which it lives and take everything to its burrow to store. Squirrels collect four times as much in provisions as they need to get through the winter. This is not because they have developed greed, which I believe only we humans possess. Squirrels have incredibly poor memories and can't find 75 percent of their supplies. When I read that, by the way, I immediately quadrupled my pencil supplies.

The San, a people in the Kalahari, spend three hours a day doing the chores necessary for their survival. They do not obtain their food from supermarkets, but rather hunt using simple means. With few natural water sources, they squeeze liquid from roots and collect dew in the morning. They work only three hours a day, albeit every day. Even figuring in weekends, vacations, and public holidays, they would still only work four and a half hours a day. However, they need neither weekends nor holidays. And they have 365 holidays a year. That's because they spend the rest of the day the way many of us would like to spend our vacation time. They chat, play with their children, and dance — a lot. And they do the work together. Except when hunting, they palaver or sing while working. They don't need psychotherapists. A colleague who is interested, like I am, in ethnopsychoanalysis (i.e., finding out what we really need and what we have lost in the course of modernization) once calculated it. He equalized our living conditions to the level the San have, namely in terms of food, clothing, and living space. Of course, he did not demand we move into straw huts in the forest and kill hares with bows and arrows. He took the real conditions of our culture as a basis and added up what food, clothing, and housing would cost at a simple level. He did not take into account goods that are not absolutely necessary for life. Even with the minimum wage, three or four and a half hours a day would be enough in our culture to achieve this standard of living. Do you doubt it? It would be about 950 euros per month.

He deliberately left out things like the "cost of the medicine man" because some values can't be compared cross-culturally. Many of our diseases are caused by civilization. The San live a healthier lifestyle and have better overall health, but that is another topic.

What I am getting at is something we call the "reality principle," which should, and must, replace the early childhood "pleasure-not pleasure principle." It probably needs no discussion that certain tasks must be performed while other activities are to be suppressed. The San, too, teach their children, in good time, to participate in the necessary tasks of the community according to their age, for example, digging for roots, and to refrain from certain other things, for example, palavering while hunting. Why don't I mention that they are not allowed to take things from others (i.e., that stealing is forbidden)? Because they don't know any concept of possession. If a San needs an object, he takes it, provided no one else is working with it at the time. Stealing would seem as absurd to them as if someone here said he stole a glass of water from a river or robbed a pine cone from the forest. The concept of ownership has only emerged in the course of modernization and is intended to secure power relations.

There is yet another phenomenon to investigate, which brings us to the third condition for self-care. All living beings have the ability to tap into reserves in threatening situations and to develop undreamt-of forces that, on occasion, even save them from grave danger. Outside of such emergency situations, these reserves are not tapped. Overall, as many studies by biologists show, nature has more reserves than those resources required for continuous functioning. Let me briefly go into this.

Work as relaxed as ants

This sounds completely absurd at first, since it's precisely these seemingly industrious little creatures that are often held up as models of tireless efficiency. This is due to a misperception a biologist uncovered a few years ago. We only see the industrious worker ants hauling things into the burrow. And we imagine it must be the same inside an ant hill. The biologist in question studied how many ants are working and how many are resting at a given time. The surprising result: Only 20 percent of the ants are working while the other 80 percent are resting. If the Indian construction crew I described in chapter 4.1 were told this, twelve would be sleeping in the ditch and two would be working. If we were to tell the ants that we have 80 percent of the population working and 20 percent resting, they would lose respect for us, provided they ever had it.

What we humans "discovered" or developed is the ability to mobilize emergency reserves even outside of crisis situations. We are the only living beings capable of demanding more from ourselves than is necessary for living, apparently without a clear goal at first. Initially, curiosity was the driving force, striving for the resolution of a question. Nothing else. The Australopithecines probably did not fantasize that humans would one day live in cities, get their drinking water from dams, and that automobiles would supersede arduous marches on foot. Just as children put a few Lego bricks on top of each other, enjoy the result, and do not think about a future meaning. Only parents often see the great architect in this.

We humans have undoubtedly achieved a lot, but we have exploited nature and ourselves in the process. Even if we now have more respect for nature, or are simply afraid that we will have to pay dearly for our environmental sins, we have not learned much in terms of self-exploitation. On the contrary, in the last twenty years, the number of burn-outs (i.e., people who have exploited themselves professionally) has risen dramatically. Almost one in two of my patients suffers from burnout or is on the verge of developing it.

Self-exploitation receives higher social recognition than self-care, which is often taken as a synonym for laziness and is referenced with barely disguised contempt. This is probably also because, in our culture, gross national product is seen as the most important measure of a nation's success and prosperity. There are other examples. While in Western cultures it's obligatory to produce as much as possible in financial value added, in Bhutan it's considered obligatory to produce as much in non-material value added as one can, meaning to promote and maintain the satisfaction of the people. Officially, the whole thing is called "gross happiness product." I think this is a faulty translation because the concept of happiness in Buddhism does not correspond to the

Western concept of happiness. A Buddhist monk is not happy when he owns a Ferrari, but when he rests contentedly within himself. That's why I use the term contentment. Personally, I take happiness to mean when I have exceeded my parking time and manage to get away undetected just before the meter attendant arrives.

Probably all people in our culture work more than they should. In doing so, we often exceed the level of necessity and do not pay attention to when we are unhealthily exploiting ourselves.

As an aside: If you think Bhutan is a backward state of goat herders and farmers, you are sorely mistaken. They have their own airline and during the COVID pandemic they were the first country in the world to have 98 percent of the adult population vaccinated, in vaccination centers whose appointments could be booked through the Ministry of Health's website.

This brings us to the next question: Why own everything? And, why does it always have to be the latest thing? Or, perhaps, why not?

5.4 Security in oneself

Security is one of the fundamental needs we humans have. When we have our basic biological needs met, such as food, sleep, and health, we want security. But I personally believe it's not really about security. I think it's about avoiding insecurity. In my experience, people suffer from insecure circumstances and then try to overcome this unpleasant state. It mainly instils fear because behind the uncertainty lurk risks or dangers that are frequently unpredictable. Security in itself does not trigger a pleasant feeling, while insecurity creates a very unpleasant one. One can well relate to the desire for safety when buying a fire extinguisher: The fire extinguisher is not bought because handling it is satisfying or because it has such a decorative appearance, but because it's supposed to make us feel protected against fire. Hand on heart: Do you know how to operate your fire extinguisher? Do you think you have the nerve to read through the operating instructions when the house is on fire?

The natural need to avoid real and basic insecurity is well understood. In the course of our cultural development, the need to avoid has expanded, as have all our needs. We no longer want to avoid only real dangers or threats but expand the field of possible threats to include possessions and circumstances that are not necessarily real threats.

At the risk of strong protest, I will give a few examples of situations that are not immediately threatening. Let's take the loss of a job. That is not really threatening. You can go on living if you are dismissed. In many countries, you are entitled to state support. Admittedly, those payments are lower than your last salary. But you will not have to starve or beg or move under the next bridge. The protest I hear is about a certain prosperity we don't want to lose. Perhaps we will have to do without the second car or the holiday, look for a smaller flat, or work in a different field.

These are not threats, they are simply restrictions. Please believe me, I don't begrudge anyone their luxuries. Oscar Wilde supposedly once said that he could do without everything but luxury. My point is different. It's not about the security of convenience, which is now so widespread in our culture. I think the central aspect is the lack of confidence in one's own abilities. I owe this realization to the two world travelers I already told you about. Through their life motto of not accepting money from others — but accepting help such as motorbike repairs or hospitality, they gained an almost unshakeable confidence in their own abilities, especially the ability to provide for their own livelihood. This conviction became strong through the many dangers they overcame.

On a side note, I have always financed my own life, even while enrolled at university. I worked in construction, in sales, as a paramedic, and as an assistant movie director. Once, when there was no "honest work," I even worked as a consultant and executive coach. It wasn't exactly pleasant because I felt disconnected from my own world and values. Still, it was a valuable learning experience.

My point is that, today, we trust more in fixed employment contracts, long tenancy agreements, and over-insurance contracts than in our own abilities. Confidence in our own abilities reduces our fears. Unfortunately, these become greater the longer we do not need our abilities because we live in security. At the same time a certain amount of uncertainty even has an invigorating effect. Why else would people stand in long lines at the new roller coaster attraction and pay a lot of money to spend a few minutes relishing uncertainty? And isn't a football match that teeters on a knife's edge and leaves us trembling until the last minute more exciting than one with a score of 6-0 after only thirty minutes?

In my psychotherapeutic practice I often deal with people who experience a severe crisis in the middle of their professional life. What looks like burn-out often turns out to be "bore-out": These people "are dying of boredom." Now, a change of work or at least of job would certainly be helpful at first glance. Unfortunately, they are often people who are civil servants, around 45 years old. They are now faced with a dilemma: either endure another twenty or more years (by which time they are likely to have accumulated a myriad of psychosomatic ailments) or dissolve their civil service employment and look for a job with more challenges. This reveals the real dilemma: They have no confidence in their own abilities.

Cultivating one's own skills and developing them further, or at least keeping them at the same level, seems more desirable to me in order to find security in one's own person. No one can deny that.

5.5 Six thousand euros are enough

My assertion that a family income of six thousand euros net per month is sufficient—and I mean more than sufficient—rarely meets with any sympathy. Most of those to whom I present this thesis find it too little. And these tend not to be those who inherently earn more. They are often people with a family income of less than three thousand euros a month. This seems to be a psychological paradox, an irrational phenomenon, for the discovery of which a social economist was once awarded the Nobel Prize. The family with an income of three thousand euros would certainly not say no to a salary increase of a thousand euros net per month. Nevertheless, everyone I have asked so far thinks that six thousand euros a month is too little.

I think this has to do with another human phenomenon.

Albert Einstein is credited with the quote: "Two things are infinite, the universe and human stupidity, but I'm not quite sure about the universe yet."

I would add a third thing: greed. (Later, I will add the need for power as a fourth).

Because apparently—this is my guess—this figure immediately triggers desires that go beyond this income sum. Suddenly three hundred euros for a meal at the Burj Al Arab (per person, of course) seems a reasonable price.

The reason we become self-indulgent is that we succumb to substitute satisfactions. And we think we must always have more of the same in order to be satisfied. Imagine you are served a tasty meal, but it contains no nutrients or only a small amount. You would enjoy it, but you would not be sated. So, you will probably order another portion—maybe there are a few calories in it, after all—and your hunger is sated a little. But not, ultimately, satisfied. It's like that with all "substitutes." Bad relationships don't get better when we have more friends.

5.6 Win-win situations

Why win-win situations make everyone happier

After all I have written, the core, the spirit of all considerations and thoughts should be to remain true to oneself and to value one's fellow human beings, the latter less for moral or Christian aspects, but more for one's own contentment. For good, satisfying relationships immediately make me more satisfied with my life. I am not talking about conformity here, but about responding to the needs and desires of others. Being responsive does not automatically mean giving in. I can fulfil someone else's wish if it also meets my needs. If that is not the case, we speak of a conflict. And conflicts frighten many people today because they confuse them with quarrels and fights and assume that there must be a winner and a loser, that one is inferior and the other oppresses the inferior. Many couples who come to me seem to believe that a balance between losing and winning establishes justice in a relationship. According to the general standards, this is also true, but our inner standards measure differently. They only count the defeats. A defeat is experienced by our unconscious as a disgrace, as a condemnation to wretchedness and is often accompanied by thoughts of revenge. In short, at this moment the relationship is disturbed, if not destroyed, for the person who feels defeated and may, with each subsequent defeat, move beyond repair.

"What about compromise?" many want to know, and they believe they have found the solution to all dilemmas. But they are wrong—even though compromise seems to be the basis of our pseudo-democratic system. "A compromise is when both are equally dissatisfied, when, in other words, the dissatisfaction is fairly distributed," I then always say. "A solution does not work like that. A real solution is when both find something that pleases them equally. And that both can agree with wholeheartedly." This is a hard road that no one prepared us for. At school we learn quite a lot of nonsensical things we never need again. Negotiation, that's the "secret" we don't learn. Negotiation means taking the other person's wishes as seriously as your own. Pressuring, blackmailing, and threatening are taboo. Anything that involves power is taboo. Seduction or offers of exchange are okay.

An example: She wants to go on holiday to Scandinavia, he is drawn to the Algarve. Possible compromises would be: Two weeks Scandinavia, two weeks Algarve. Or this year Algarve, next Scandinavia. Someone will always be dissatisfied. And probably nagging. "But maybe he will like the beauty of Scandinavia." "Yes, but only maybe." Pretty risky, isn't it? The most stupid form of compromise would be to take a ruler, put it between Oslo and Faro, and take the exact middle, let's say, Belgium. Then both are equally unhappy (nothing against Belgium, but Belgium was never under consideration).

Many colleagues who also do couples therapy are of the opinion that couples need a "culture of conflict." Even though this seems to be an almost irrefutable principle, I have to strongly disagree.

Arguing is always destructive. It is primarily about harming the other person, not about a constructive solution to the problem. While one person is still talking—probably ranting or hurling hateful tirades—the other is not listening at all, but thinking up new nastiness and venom, loading his verbal cannons.

The solution is debate. Couples, but also groups, society and politics need a culture of debate (that's why I spoke of pseudo-democracy earlier), but it has to be a mature and true debate. At best, we have learned this at home, when our own parents or patchwork parents have mastered it. But who can say that about themselves?

What would a good (i.e., a mature and fair) discussion look like? Both could ask the other what is so important to them about their idea, what fascinates her, for example, about Scandinavia and him about the Algarve. Both could tell each other stories, talk about experiences, show pictures, watch documentaries and so on. Seducing is always allowed, since the seduced always has the option to say no.

An important point not taken into account in disputes: Decisions need time. You and the other have to let what you have heard and seen sink in, sleep on it, talk about it with a friend, and sleep on it again. Many people today can no longer stand this tension. If things don't move fast enough, pressure is exerted, and a quick pseudo-solution is made over the knee. Most of the time, the "Jell-O is nailed to the wall."

Only those who are really convinced — or could be convinced — will stand behind their decision 100 percent. This makes it difficult at first, but easy afterwards. Instead of the other way round.

6. Self-sabotage

6.1 Possession

Why do you always have to own everything — and why does it always have to be the latest thing?

I won't hide the fact that I like to write with well-functioning laptops, and I write many of my thoughts in a Moleskine, the Mercedes Benz among notebooks. A little luxury is allowed. I'm not going to instruct anyone in ascetic renunciation. Strictly speaking, I consider ascetic renunciation a form of Western luxury with a complacent attitude toward poorer or needy people. Moreover, asceticism can also become an addiction. I will only point out the mechanisms that inevitably lead us to a possessive attitude. You may continue to order a new mobile phone every year. But you may also lose the desire for it after this chapter, because you question the point of it.

Sonab and I are sitting in the Zanskar valley by an artificial lake. I want to know something about the importance of irrigation and how the tasks are distributed. Sonab is more interested in my digital camera. Not a particularly expensive model. Just lightweight and with small batteries I can easily charge with my solar panel at 3,500 meters, because there is no electricity here. I can see it in Sonab's shining eyes that he would like to own the camera. For a moment, I am overcome with the idea of giving it to him; I would just take out the memory card. But then I have doubts. He would not have a memory card, and he would also be missing the solar panel. I could certainly do without that—but what would he do with the pictures? He doesn't have a laptop or a PC. No resident owns such a thing. And the nearest photo lab that could make digital prints is about seven hundred kilometers away. This brings to mind a family with a dubious reputation in the village. They have a television and a DVD player. Is there a TV station there? No. Neither is there a video store or a shop that sells DVDs. And the family doesn't own any DVDs either. The TV and DVD player have been placed in a conspicuous place in the living area.

That's how we get to the bottom of envy. Both that family and I possess something no one else has. This creates a desire for possession in us humans that is hard to overlook, apparently fed by envy. I say apparently because I believe there is another mechanism behind it. We all do not want to be on the fringe of the community, and above all not to be ridiculed, treated in a lowly manner, or laughed at because we do not own something. Or perhaps we own something that is less valued in the value system of this community (e.g., a six-year-old mobile phone or clothes that do not come from a so-called brand company). Most people don't ask themselves whether they even need the possessions that others have, and they don't ask whether the new model really gives them personal advantages.

Feeling inferior to others has a counterpart: feeling superior to others.

6.2 Playing a Role

... makes people dissatisfied — and ill

People must adapt. To the environment, to their environment, to social circumstances, to working conditions, to the needs of other people who are important to them, and so on. Deep in their personalities, most people are considerate creatures who value and enjoy social interaction in groups as much as intimacy, togetherness, and protection in smaller relationship structures. Nevertheless, I would like to draw attention to the phenomenon of over-adaptation, because many people adapt themselves beyond what is necessary and, in so doing, often not only forego freedoms to which they are naturally entitled but also deny important parts of their personality. They bend themselves until they play a role, instead of living their own life — a life that includes their specific characteristics, rough edges and all — aspects of their personality that do not always make them popular.

In my opinion, over-conformity is an expression of a limiting attitude. This only arises through an ongoing and ever-increasing over-adaptation and self-denial, until the over-adapted person himself believes he is the way he is of his own free will. But the denial cannot be maintained indefinitely, since while the needs are repressed into the unconscious, they will still seek liberation and realization. One only has to pay attention to the nightly dreams of these people to learn what a banished part of their person really wants. And this doesn't only affect the psyche of this person at night. He also has to endure many inner conflicts during the day when he is "tempted." Here our psyche helps itself with some mechanisms only meant for emergencies—like first aid kits and fire extinguishers. For one thing, such people—who are, in reality, unhappy—split off the needs and personality traits they forbid themselves and "park" them with others. We say they "project" the forbidden parts into others and shift the inner conflict into an outer one. Because it's "easier" to fight others or to distance oneself from them with a sniff. A second protective mechanism for maintaining the static of the self-invented cloud cuckoo home is to seek protection in a strong or large community of like-minded people. In this way, they not only secure support, even if it's only virtual, but also reinforce their, in reality, fragile attitude toward life through the strength or mass of their "equals." And this brings us to a phenomenon: the lonesome wolf, the bird of paradise, the individualist can't be sure of such support. He has to muster a great deal of fear tolerance and risks having only a few people around him who think and feel the same way as he does. This is where many people encounter a primal human fear: the fear of being alone. They fear being so crazy, so against the current, that they will be rejected by everyone. This fear is anchored in our primal biological mechanisms, like the infant's fear of starving to death if the mother is not immediately at hand. The fear of being alone is never entirely justified. It can happen that you are suddenly the only one in a group who has an opinion. But that doesn't last. No human being is so individual that there is not at least one other person who "ticks" similarly. In psychotherapy, many patients lose unsatisfactory relationships. I deliberately say "lose" because the process is usually very quiet and without confrontation. Sometimes my patients are frightened by the "de-cluttering" of their social circle, but ultimately discover that the few that remain bring in satisfying contacts. It is like clearing counterfeit money out of one's wallet. What remains has real value.

However, it's also interesting that such nonconformist people are officially admired rather than rejected. The protagonists in magazines, books, and films are not conformist people. A series about the uneventful, everyday life of a well-behaved and contour-less accountant is unlikely to attract an audience. This is also a psychological coping mechanism: The hidden or forbidden desires and facets of the personality are, as we say, "delegated" to others. Or they're relegated to our daydreams. So, the accountant may dream of being an explorer or becoming a hero for a moment, risking his life to save others. Here we get on the trail of two other phenomena: the fear of one's own actions and the unwillingness of many people to take responsibility for their actions, for their personality, and for their life.

Fear is a universal phenomenon that (presumably) all living beings know in some form. Its purpose is to protect us from destruction or harm, which is why it's necessary for life. But not all fear is useful. Often our fears hinder us more than they protect us. Fear of approaching an attractive person for whom one has developed tender feelings may protect one from the cold shower of rejection, but it prevents one from developing a satisfying relationship in the long run. Many think such fears have to be "overcome." I am skeptical about this and would rather say they need to be examined. It's unavoidable to take a risk now and then — a calculable one. I consciously take the risk that a desired person will reject me. Of course, that scratches my ego. The calculation is that I cannot please everyone or anyone. This makes development possible instead of stagnation.

I see a danger in "overcoming" fears as this is often confused with a dangerous counter-steering. The person with a fear of heights then climbs high buildings, for example, and walks on the edge. In doing so, the fear is not subjected to a test but is forcibly bypassed and thus not overcome. In my experience, fears can only be "overcome" (i.e., brought down to a realistic level) if they are tested, step by step, and the fear increasingly gives way to courage through positive experiences. Such as when the person with the fear of heights gradually goes up one floor at a time and, I think this is important, develops a sense of when self-care should kick in. A lecturer of mine has crossed the Atlantic alone on two occasions: once in a folding boat and once in a dugout canoe carved by natives. He says he overcame his fear through autogenic training. I think he suppressed his fear with autogenic training and had a huge portion of luck. Every year, about two hundred so-called single-handed sailors "disappear," despite the most modern technical equipment. The sea and high altitudes remain dangerous for us humans — we are neither fish nor birds.

Nevertheless, fear should be checked down to a healthy level. We no longer live in a time when we risk a live-fire burial as soon as we don't go with the flow. And this brings us to the next chapter: why courage is important.

But first we should look at another human survival mechanism that can be life-saving in extreme psychological situations, but which, in the case of over-adaptation, exacerbates the unhealthy effects of adaptation. I call this mechanism the "camp effect," related to the Stockholm syndrome; people who involuntarily fall into the hands of henchmen support them after some time of oppression. In some cases, for example, prisoners tried to make friends with the worst concentration camp guards. This seems paradoxical, as if pigs were helping the butcher sharpen the knives. Yet this act of adaptation makes perfect sense—even if it did no more than help many in the Nazi era to prolong their lives somewhat. This reflexive psychological reaction of humans is similar to the play dead or submission reflex of many animals. A dog that throws itself on its back shows its attacker it surrenders and no longer poses a threat, since the attacker could kill it at any time. The attacker no longer fears the other could become dangerous to him. Of course, this attitude can change overnight, the subjugated can draw new strength and attack again. To signal that this will not be the case, the subjugated shows the attacker that he agrees with him, that he thinks what he's doing is right. We say: He identifies with the attacker. This can be a good protection, in the camp situation probably the only sensible, often last option the victim has to react. Friends and supposed comrades-in-arms are not attacked as often as oppositional or undiscerning people.

6.3 Superiority

Why superiority harms others

Superiority over others seems to be an inherent part of our culture, already exerting its appeal in children's games. Why shouldn't we be allowed to enjoy ourselves when we have won at Monopoly, captured the heart of the one we, eliminated our rival, got a place at university, or snatched away someone's dream job? I don't want to take away anyone's enjoyment of having achieved something. One is allowed to be happy, that's not in question. However, I see danger in humiliating the other person. The word loser immediately comes to mind — that's how much the inhumane, performance-driven, capitalist society, which mercilessly jumps around with fellow human beings and the environment, has already shaped us. "Loser" is a swear word that degrades and dehumanizes the targeted person. The word makes them inferior creatures who are denied any dignity and deserve no respect. But if one looks at one's "victory" in a more differentiated way, and not absolutely but relatively, then one's own glamour melts away and the "competitors" are automatically seen in a different light, namely, in their literal meaning as fellow runners, running together. It's important to always consider the circumstances in which one was superior to the other. If my parents are educated, psychologically-halfway stable people and have always lovingly encouraged and challenged me, my A grade might be worth less than the hard-won C of someone who grew up in an environment where alcohol, emotional neglect, and experiences of violence played a formative role.

The most important things that hold us humans together are our bonds and mutual appreciation. Without mutual appreciation, relationships are not sustainable in the long run. With my contempt for a person who was perhaps inferior to me in a certain situation or discipline, I destroy the relationship with him. Even if he follows me in masochistic admiration, this is not an authentic relationship based on mutual affection and equal esteem. It's possible the other person is only packaging his anger and thoughts of revenge into the apparent allegiance and idealization of my person. Better said, he "parks" them until the moment has come to break out of the role. The vernacular has well recognized this form of lying, hypocritical behavior and calls it "shit friendly." The kind words are not honey, as they seem at first, but made of feces.

And that's where none of us should end up—neither on one side nor the other. We certainly wouldn't break a sweat if we signaled to someone who was inferior to us that we value them as a person. That's what we do with friends. Who would ridicule a good friend after beating him in tennis?

6.4 Disrespect

Why respect for others is important and disrespect for others harms ourselves

Why is respect so important? Actually, we have already figured that out. The word is written on footballers' jerseys, in the stadiums, so "writ large". Officially. But respect cannot be enforced if one's own reasons for disrespect have not been thought through, worked through, and overcome. If a white person has a disrespectful opinion toward non-white people, he will not lose it by being forbidden to use or criticized for using racist language. This is an unconscious obfuscation tactic, a diversionary maneuver designed to hide a ubiquitous problem, namely, that we all commit such "sins" of dehumanization. The fight for "correct" gendering or other forms of skirmishes to achieve apparent equality not infrequently belie the fact that our disdain and disrespect run far deeper than we would like to admit. Before you take me to the moral scaffold, take a look at the label of the shirt or trousers you are wearing. Where does it come from? Under what conditions was it made? Who made the "big profit" from it?

Respect for the environment

Soon, at least before the end of this century, humans want to fly to Mars. And after the flight to the moon, the motive behind this is not pure research interest. No, this time they want to start populating Mars—to colonize it. Even if this time the colonization causes little damage in the target area, one wonders what the whole thing is about, unless one is completely intoxicated by human megalomania and its infinite desires. I can still understand curiosity. But an escape from Earth? Have we already given up on the planet? The nine-month journey is supposed to cost 22 billion euros to send six people in a lead box the size of a camper van to the red planet. To all leftists who just got moist eyes: Red doesn't refer to the political sentiments on Mars, but to its physical color radiation.

Cost per passenger: 8.3 million euros. Have I miscalculated? No, just converted to "realistic." Suppose we were to relocate everyone to Mars and Condor or Ryanair were to offer cheap flights. And let's say they could offer one-way tickets for eighty thousand euros (1 percent of the current price); the resettlement of eleven billion—in 2100!—would cost a whopping 880 trillion euros. If we assume IKEA has kindly donated the little houses on Mars, or the new Martian residents are fond of roasting in the nude, the whole project would "only" devour twice the projected world gross domestic product in 2100. Cut back a bit for two or three years, a trait people are known to find very easy, and we will have gotten everyone there. In 2021, world GDP was approximately 85 trillion, and it's expected to increase by 40 trillion every ten years. Unfortunately, forecasts have an unpleasant characteristic: They are usually wrong. I could list tons more inconsistencies—What are we doing up there? How does a Martian economy work? (Incidentally, why Jeff Bezos wants to go there is already clear to me.)

I plead to preserve our really very beautiful and livable planet. And to use our money, time, energy, and brainpower for this more realistic goal.

And, if Jeff Bezos still wants to go up there, I'll be happy to donate something for the purpose. Provided he doesn't come back.

6.5 Carelessness

You don't need to buy mindfulness; you get it as a gift

Many patients ask me, "Can you tell me how to learn mindfulness quickly?" Of course I can, although quick and mindful may seem like irreconcilable contradictions. "Turn off the car radio." Or the mobile phone. "That's it?" some ask skeptically. But that's more than one might think at first glance. It's not only the first and necessary step in the right direction, it's already the path. Leave out everything that distracts. When voices or instruments from outside stop beseeching us, we can hear our inner voice. Suddenly, inner images, fantasies, and ideas arise. This is exactly how psychoanalysis works, when done properly. Don't think hard about heavy topics or the past, the relationship with parents or siblings, but just feel. "Tell me what is on your mind. Whether it seems important or appropriate, whether it seems embarrassing and childish. Everything is welcome." That's my basic rule. Every psychoanalyst has his or her own recipe. At first, patients find it difficult to surrender to their inner voice. But this is the only way to get to the repressed, buried, switched off, and otherwise mothballed, buried, or rusty sides of one's being. I often compare the process with the restoration of a historic house, an old mural, or a classic car. Our usual tools of acceleration are not only of little help here, but they actually do more harm than good. The excavator or the concrete mixer will not be able to restore the old timber frame to its original condition. Paint spray guns will ruin the old painting, and the sledgehammer would ruin the rusted side door. It takes patience. And aimlessness. This is what the wise British psychoanalyst Wilfred Bion demanded of his colleagues: "No desire," no intention, no goal should the analyst have when listening to the patient.

It was a few years ago, but I still remember it as if it were yesterday. I like to walk through the forest in order to reconnect with myself. On this day, I was drawn to the Kreuzberg, a hill in Bonn. There's an old chapel there. For some reason, I always have to take a look inside. Maybe I want to make sure nothing has changed. The musty smell, the old benches—there's something reassuring about some things staying the way they are for hundreds of years. Like the round kiosk from my childhood in 1950s style, where children still buy sweets or grab bags.

This time something was different, but that didn't worry me. A woman was sitting in front of one of the old murals. She had a painter's palette in one hand and in the other she held a brush whose bristle head was barely recognizable and probably consisted only of a few badger hairs. With this brush she painted the finger of one of the people in the picture. She dabbed very lightly on her palette, mixed a new shade there, and tested it on her left palm before applying the paint to the painting's index finger. I was fascinated, sat down on one of the old marble steps, and watched her spellbound. She'd certainly noticed me but didn't let my presence disturb her. She probably sensed I would not ask her silly questions or make stupid comments. Above all, her hands captivated me. I had forgotten the time and was taken with every new brush stroke. Perhaps others would have asked themselves or the restorer with the graceful hand movements how long it would take her to finish. I must admit that hands fascinate me. As a psychotherapist, I pay a lot of attention to my patients' hands, how they move, what they do when they are tense, and so on. And I pay attention to the handshake. That often gives me the first clues about what's going on inside the patient as soon as I greet them. Maybe I'll write a book about it one day. But I think it would be better not to, because then the magic could be lost.

At some point, the restorer turned to me. Her "hello" told me, judging by her accent, that she was probably from Poland. A conversation in English is a damned poor prerequisite for people who have a different mother tongue, if one wants to continue, in a dignified way, the sensuality that has arisen in a certain space. Alas, sensual conversations are something great, fulfilling. I remarked that she must have a lot of patience. Her confounded face told me I had said something banal, as if I had told a fish it probably needed a lot of water. What a foolish remark. She didn't need patience. She was one with the work. It didn't matter how long it took to finish the finger, the hand, the whole body of the saint, the whole fresco. Her activity had something existentialist about it. It was her task, her sensuality, her happiness. She was one with the brush, one with the paint, with the sacred. There were no boundaries, she was completely in the here and now.

The next time you see something being restored, watch for a while. The best thing to do is to shut up and, at most, bring the artist a cup of tea. Dry church air often makes you thirsty.

7. Becoming human

7.1 Respect for the weak

Being weak or showing weakness does not enjoy a good reputation in our culture. The strong, preferably the winner, is the one recognized. The loser is laughed at with pity. Appreciating the weak is just as important, though in our success-oriented, technical, and profit-oriented capitalist culture it's no longer common. Yet we were all weak once — when we were babies, when we were children. And we are often weak in adulthood as well. When we are ill, when we are in despair, when we have failed to achieve something, or when fate throws a monkey wrench in the works. Or when — as in my case — the groundwaters of doubt creep up my foundation walls from time to time. And when we are old and frail. I often wonder what those über-cool hipsters and start- up-winner types look like at eighty. Did they beat all their rivals before and now have no friends? Or does nobody want to know anything about them anymore because they are no longer young, dynamic, and successful? Respect for the weak and being supportive corresponds with our need to help others. We humans like to do this, and do it well, because it's satisfying. The reward is not only gratitude, or the gleam in the eyes of others, but also the gleam in our own eyes. Unfortunately, the rejection of the weak corresponds with the denial of one's own weaknesses and often also with fear of one's own need for help, of the triumph of the superior, of mockery or contempt by our fellow human beings. Do we really want to live in a society where the weak are rejected, marginalized? There is another way.

Christmas Eve, a pleasantly cool day in Funabashi. The spectators at the Nakayama Racecourse look forward to the race. Christmas Eve is horse racing day in Japan. And everyone is waiting for the star of the evening, the mare Haru Urara, which translates as "Lovely Spring." Why is Haru Urura the star of the evening? Because Haru Urara has given the same consistent performance in the last hundred races: She has lost all of them, always finished last. Haru Urara is the star because she always competes and always struggles. The Japanese appreciate the fighter more than the winner.

Personally, I would like to see a society, a culture, in which attitude counts more than success. At least, the successes that are considered successes in our culture.

7.2 Time and patience

Many people fail in their projects for two reasons. Either they have set themselves too many goals or too little time. Usually both.

When I want to travel, I have developed an effective ritual for myself: I pack clothes and money in the suitcase. Then I close it, open it again, and put the clothes and money on my bed. Now I halve the clothes and double the money. I do the same with my projects: halve the goals, double the time.

I mean the period of time in which I believe I can realize something. Otherwise, it's advisable to work like the ants, which I described in chapter 5.3. Socioeconomically, this is also known as the Pareto principle, or the 80/20 rule. Wilfried Fritz Pareto, an Italian universal genius, found that it takes 20 percent of one's time and energy to get one thing done 80 percent. To achieve the last 20 percent, that is, to get a task or project 100 percent done, you need the remaining 80 percent of your strength and time. Think about how you created your last PowerPoint presentation. It was ready after two hours. It took eight hours to find, edit, insert, and adjust a few silly jokes or semi-hilarious little pictures. And in the presentation, you need 20 percent of your time and energy to convey 80 percent of the content. You need the remaining 80 percent of your time and energy to prevent the audience from falling asleep—because of the silly jokes and sleep-inducing pictures you have put in with so much effort.

Something for the perfectionists among you: Is there a step up from perfect? Yes, there is. The improvement on "perfect" is "finished".

In software production, however, the principle does not apply. This is due to the stubbornness of these tin brains. Therefore, the 90/90 rule applies here: A programmer needs 90 percent of his time (and gummy bears) to complete 90 percent of a program. Since he can't stop at this point because of his stubbornness — the computer would not manage much more than 0 percent of the tasks it's supposed to do — he has to manage the missing 10 percent as well. And for this it needs the remaining 90 percent of its time (and gummy bears).

7.3 Slowness

Texas, the United States of America: I'm sitting in a restaurant. A hectically moving, obviously completely overwhelmed waitress takes my order. She not only wants to know the starter and main course, but also whether I want a dessert and coffee to go with it. I never know at the beginning of the meal. Maybe I'll be too full, maybe I'll be nauseous and lying on the floor retching, or maybe I'll want something different from what I chose at the beginning. "Cindy" is written on the tag of her apron uniform. Cindy is tense. She doesn't seem to enjoy the work. Perhaps she is also annoyed by such an indecisive guest. I'm robbing her of precious time. I wonder if she already has an ulcer. "Thanks, no, no dessert, no coffee." Cindy writes everything down on a small pad and runs off. "Cindy, don't you want to know what credit card I'm going to use to pay?" I want to ask, but swallow the sentence. She's stressed enough. The tall man at the next table has apparently overheard our brief interaction (but hopefully not read my mind); he gives me a grim look, then digs into his hamburger as if there were a Guinness Book competition going on. I wonder whether I might get shot for a harmless joke – by Cindy or by "Jim," that's what I call the grim guy at the next table. I notice Jim is wearing his Texas hat while eating. I look around. All the men have their hats on. All the hats are the same; they only differ in slight shades of color. Are they afraid someone might steal their hat or get it mixed up? After all, a Stetson costs about three hundred dollars. No, that would probably get you twenty-five years in a Texan jail—without parole.

Before I can think any further, Cindy interrupts me. With an uncharitable "Here we go," she deposits my coleslaw on the table. At the next table, Jim has polished off his dessert and poured the coffee down his throat, while, with his other hand, he has thrown the money for the bill onto the plate with the bill. He leaves the restaurant in a hurry. Waiting for the change? No time. Then I suddenly realize: Taking off and putting on the hats again takes time. A lot of time. While Cindy snatches the plate for the main course away from me with a grim look (at the next table, where Jim was just sitting, "Jack" is already paying his bill while finishing off his coffee in big gulps. I can see that I am holding up the business unnecessarily), I conclude my calculations regarding Texas hats: At 16 years of age, when the Texan skull is fully grown, the young men get their Stetson, which they keep on for the rest of their lives. This saves them 141.94 hours, almost six days of their lives. No idea what they do with the time they save.

"Here we go," the bill flies onto my table. What Cindy meant, of course, was "Here you go." She wants to get rid of me. It's mutual. Instead of the usual 15 percent, I give her a 25 percent tip, for a total of 25 dollars—luckily it was not an expensive restaurant. I owe this lesson to my culture. May the good people of Texas forgive me for being used as an a foil in this chapter.

7.4 First things first

I sit at my desk. There is a lot to do: countless emails to answer; the tax consultant to call (I look forward to this as I do a root canal); bills to pay; checking beforehand whether I haven't already paid them; an event to prepare; talking to the venue manager about the seating (U-shape, O-shape or parliamentary?); calling the technician to see if the setup went well; answer new emails. In short: all that unbearable shit.

Oh, yes: finally pay the sales tax. Do I still have the money? The VAT always disappears in an inexplicable way. I've always wanted to clear this up with the tax office, but they're not interested in finding the cause; they just want the money. It doesn't help to say the VAT hasn't disappeared, that someone else has it, to suggest they take it from him. Money is only ever a guest, never a permanent tenant. Most of the time it's just a flying visit. It comes in the door, says "hello," and disappears over the balcony. Often, I don't even have time to return the greeting. My tax advisor, the world's most unhedonistic pain in the behind, thinks it might be "because the balcony door is always wide open." I have no idea what he means by that. Surely one is allowed to air the room a little. Maybe I'll invite the man from the sales tax office over one day. Then he can sit down on my sofa and try to snatch the money. "We're looking for your money from the previous year," says the tax investigator. "Great!" I reply, "be sure to let me know when you've found it."

I'm firmly convinced there are not only holes in my wallet, but also time holes or wormholes (no idea which term is the right one) on my desk and in my apartment. In any case, the holes are there, that much is certain. I put something on the desk and the next day it's gone. I'm not talking only about pens or pencils, those automatically dematerialize, turn into energy and are gone forever, or empty or broken. I search everywhere; I search myself to death. Can't find it, no matter what I do. Miraculously, the object or letter or whatever reappears after a few weeks, often exactly where I thought I had put it. It was just in a different time dimension. How could I be so stupid as to put it exactly in a wormhole?

You see, writing is more fun for me than making calls and transfers. "The tax consultant is no longer in the house? Not back until Monday? What a pity." Good thing his assistant can't see my grin. "Dear tax office clerk, how great would have been my pleasure—and I am sure yours too—if I could have proudly announced to you today that the long overdue VAT is on its way to you by a hefty transfer. Unfortunately, this didn't happen as expected, a circumstance that is solely due to the retentive, pecuniary inhibition and unyielding stubbornness of the bank that refuses to extend my overdraft. Regrettably, another circumstance, through no fault of my own, also prevents immediate payment. For today, I was expecting a not inconsiderable royalty payment from my publisher. Although this payment was received, it was disproportionately low. According to my publisher, this is due to the readers who simply don't want to buy my books. You will certainly notice: We are both in the same boat, both waiting for our money. Shouldn't we join forces? I would like to take this opportunity to ask you: How many employees does your tax office have? And how many of your colleagues don't yet have a copy of my new book? Tell me the number, and I'll bring you the copies right away. You can all pay the money into the tax office under my tax number. Yours sincerely..."

Parliamentary form? O-shape? U-shape? "Make it X-shape!" "Excuse me, how do you do that?" "You're a meeting room provider, you'll work it out. Talk to you later."

If I do what I enjoy first, I get in a good mood. And I get creative. Today, I invented the 1/50 principle: With 1 percent of time and effort, you can do everything 50 percent. I tried it out right away with emails:

"Dear Mr. Adler, we would like to enquire whether you will be available as agreed blah, blah, blah, next Saturday at 3:00 p.m. blah, blah, blah. Please give us until blah, blah blah, blah."

The 1 percent answer: "Yes."

"Dear Dieter, have you gotten around to blah, blah, blah yet, I would absolutely blah, blah. Why don't you tell me when blah, blah."

The 1 percent answer: "No, soon."

7.5 Modesty and humility

"We can only do our work in humility and modesty," a supervisor admonished and comforted me many years ago when a treatment had gone fundamentally wrong. Failed treatments are something psychotherapists take very much to heart. The treatment was a long time ago, but his words have stuck, etched deeply into my personality.

It is humanly understandable: We all want to break out of our natural insignificance. Even if it's only once: to shine, to be admired by others, to be the center of attention, to be at the top. When we lived in manageable small groups, this was still relatively easy. You proved yourself courageous in the hunt, caught a particularly big fish all by yourself, constructed something clever, or bravely faced an enemy. The areas in which recognition is achieved seem to be mostly of an original masculine nature. Female achievements are probably taken more for granted—but that's another topic, which certainly deserves closer consideration.

In the ever-expanding fields of life, recognition in the small group counts less and less; the standards for valuing an achievement as exceptional rise ever higher. This means efforts to achieve recognition become increasingly difficult and demanding. At the same time, the likelihood of failure increases as well, along with frustration, which in turn leads many to want to undo the disgrace—the opposite of the hoped-for shine in the eyes of others—often by even more ambitious efforts with the risk of further and probably greater frustration. A vicious circle that often leads to ever greater self-devaluation, combined with the fact that one's existing skills are no longer valued at all.

By chasing recognition and the glimmer in the eyes of others, we lose respect for our own personality with all its abilities, good sides, and lovable qualities. In short: The splendor of one's own person lies in its uniqueness. And no one can take that away from us.

Trophies, VIP stands, honor and glory, however, can.

"His first arrow shot out of the brightness into the deep night. I recognized from the impact that it had hit the target. The second arrow also hit the target.

When I had turned on the light at the target stand, I discovered to my dismay that the first arrow was sitting in the middle of the black, while the second had splintered the notch of the first arrow and slashed the shaft a bit before drilling into the black next to it. I didn't dare pull the arrows out one by one, but brought them back together with the target. The master scrutinized them closely. "The first shot," he said, "was no trick, you will think, because I have been so familiar with my target for decades, that I must know where it is even in the deepest darkness. That may be, and I won't try to talk myself out of it. But the second arrow that hit the first — what do you think of that? I, for one, know that it was not 'I' who should be credited with that shot. 'It' took a shot and 'it' hit. Let us bow to the target as to the Buddha!"

Eugen Herrigel: Zen in the Art of Archery,
Vintage Spiritual Classics, 1999
[orig. published by Barth, Munich 1987]

7.6 The meaning of life

The meaning of life has an almost magical significance for most of us. For those who indulge in more superficial pleasures and perhaps don't want to pursue more profound or sustainable goals, the choice is simple. They indulge unconditionally in hedonism.

For the majority of people, the question of meaning is nevertheless a very serious matter that compels them for a long time, perhaps never losing its hold on them. Even children search for an answer. And if no answer materializes, many suffer from their self-certified meaninglessness or the indeterminacy of their own being. Closely connected to this, or so it seems to me, is the question of one's own imprint on world history. Everyone would like to leave their mark on the world—preferably on the whole universe—and somehow remain alive at least in the memory of others. In some cases, unfortunately, even through bad actions. Thankfully, those are in the minority.

If we do not find a sufficient answer, which, as a child, is impossible in large part due to the lack of experience with the world, we try to get answers from others. Many people look for mentors whom, in a state of constant self-doubt, they elevate to the status of charismatic gurus, which is fatal to their own search for meaning and personality development.

First, the sobering answer from me: The meaning of life exists as no more than does the philosopher's stone. The desire for a universally valid solution or formula insulates us from the unpleasant truth that finding the meaning of one's own life takes great effort. That's why psychotherapy is arduous and painful— it's an arduous confrontation with one's own person. There's no other way to find the meaning of one's own life. But I believe that other errors and misconceptions complicate the search. For one thing, we have to deal with our inner conflicts. Do I want to be a "good" person who helps others, or do I want to pursue a career where I may have to be ruthless to succeed? But it's not only these ethical conflicts that complicate our choices. Even if we choose a side, let's say "the good one," many questions remain unanswered: Should I study medicine, theology, or psychology? Should I help people here or in a developing country? What do I do if my partner has a different disposition? What if my family or other people important to me don't agree with my choice and turn away from me?

The self-created difficulty lies in the Western mistaken belief that a solution must always be unique, uncomplicated, or valid for all eternity. This latter expectation seems to me to be the most difficult circumstance or pitfall.

In my eyes, the way out of the misery seems to be, on the one hand, to broaden the field. No one would seriously consider that they have to find "the optimal dish" that they would then want to eat every day for the rest of their lives. We always decide on such things according to the situation. We look at the menu and let our unconscious find what our palate has the greatest appetite for today, here and now. For the same reason, incidentally, I reject fixed appointments and bookings, or try to avoid them as much as possible.

In the course of my life, I've had so many professions that, on the surface, had nothing to do with each other: paramedic, local editor at the daily newspaper, radio reporter, educational consultant, filmmaker, writer, assistant director, director, film producer, executive coach, documentary film maker, programmer, database developer, psychotherapist, psychoanalyst, group psychotherapist, supervisor, and managing director. I gave up a training course to become a professional pilot after my first solo flying lesson. This was fortunate, because that job is (for me at least) deadly boring, as computers do all the work. Only take-off, landing, and emergency situations require the pilot's intervention, but an emergency is the last thing pilots wish for—unless their name is Antoine de Saint-Exupéry.

Today, I know there was something good and right for me in each of these professions, even if I would have preferred to do without certain experiences. But one usually only knows that afterward. Just like with a meal—the cook's understanding of "not too spicy" can be different from that of the stomach.

It comes down to a certain diversity of available options to choose from or narrow down, depending on one's perspective. Like a toolbox you pack and keep for life. As anyone who is skilled in handicrafts knows, universal tools are usually useless. I am thinking of special kitchen appliances that can do everything—chop, strain, cook, bake, and who knows what else. Before the last instalment has been paid, they are stored in the kitchen cupboard for about two decades before being sent to their preliminary final destination: the flea market, where they find a new interim collector for ten to twenty euros.

Let us move on to the next error: a temporally unlimited validity of the question of meaning. One could also say the desire for a static solution. The desire for permanence is understandable but, unfortunately, ill-advised. Genuine solutions should, indeed I believe must, be dynamic. An ideal I held at twenty years of age can and will look very different at thirty. It has evolved. And with this, we can also quickly dispel another misconception. We tend to define development as "development toward something better," or at least something positive, whereby the weighting is always a subjective one: The development of rents, for example, has a contrary, diametrically opposed connotation for tenants as opposed to landlords.

Therefore, I would like to propose a neutral definition of development: Development is a change of an existing state into another, just like a river modifying its course over time. It doesn't make the change on its own initiative, but adapts to new conditions.

7.7 What is happiness?

So what does real happiness mean?

Actually, we should know that by now. For myself, I've come to the following conclusions:

1. Happiness is sitting together with others, with a group of like-minded people in a relaxed setting, being in peaceful contact with each other. And the best thing is to be able to present yourself as you are, to be authentic. That's my top priority.
2. Helping other people is a great happiness because we like to do it. Ideally, we do it altruistically (i.e., without getting anything in return and without ending up on the front page as heroes). I myself have saved the lives of four people (to my knowledge, in any case). Not as a psychotherapist, but in a threatening situation that almost ended fatally. I was astounded when one of these four knocked on my door years later and thanked me. I was very touched by this, but I never expected it. It's enough to have the feeling in the evening that you've helped another person.
3. Doing something good for others brings happiness. Giving something makes the giver at least as happy as the receiver—provided you hit on the right thing. It's similar to helping. The only difference is that helping is an indeterminate product of chance that I can't intentionally bring about. I can give a gift at any time.

But there are also states of happiness we can experience just with ourselves. I find the highest happiness when I am in contact with myself. That's just as important as being in contact with others. We need both: contact with others and contact with ourselves. It's especially satisfying when I get exactly what I need at the moment, when I feel like being in contact with others, and they have the time and the desire to do so at that very moment.

The same is true when I feel my own self in moments of silence, when I gain access to feelings that have been buried by the turmoil and noise of everyday life and professional and private challenges, and the feelings become ever quieter with each new sedimentary layer of reality. When I can be alone, the wind of silence blows away the sand of everyday life. And, little by little, I can feel myself again; I have contact with myself again in the clear evening air of silence; I am one with myself again.

Getting in touch with others in this way is also one of the moments of happiness that we humans are naturally capable of, something that is inherent in us.

Namibia, 2015, August. It's winter. An anthropologist, whose name has slipped my mind because I was annoyed with her beyond measure, leads us to the Himbaoganda. This oganda — as the Ovahimba call their villages — lies hidden in the dense woodland of the savannah of the Kaokoveld in northern Namibia above the Etosha Pan. The anthropologist tells me to go ahead. Then, out of nowhere, two little boys, about five and seven years old, approach me from the left. They are two beautiful children. And I don't know why, but I hold out my hands to them. It just happened that way. They came to me and each of them grabbed one of my hands. Together, the two of them led me into the village. I have never before experienced this feeling that suddenly poured out of me from within, and therefore have no words for it. A state as if I no longer existed, but not because I or my ego had dissolved, but because deep inside, I had suddenly merged with everything—and, seemingly paradoxically, experienced an unprecedented sense of freedom. Please do not go to the Kaokoveld. You must find the Kaokoveld within yourself.

Literature

Adler, D. (1991): Crisis Management: Coping with Stress in Solving Complex Problems, unpublished.

Erikson, Erik H. (1959): Identity and the Life Cycle. Norton & Company; Revised Edition (1994)

Herrigel, E. (1987): Zen in the art of archery. Munich. Barth. English translation: Zen in the Art of Archery, Vintage Spiritual Classics, 1999

Klein, M. (2001): The soul life of the infant and other contributions to psychoanalysis. Stuttgart. Klett-Cotta.

Kohut, H. (1979): The healing of the self. Frankfurt am Main. Suhrkamp.

Mahler, M.; Pine, F.; Bergman, A. (1980): The psychic birth of man. Frankfurt am Main. Fischer.

Metz, C.; Schubert, K. (1999): Abgefahren: Around the world in 16 years. Cologne. KiWi.

Shepher, J. (1983): Incest - A Biopsychological View. New York et al. Academic Press.

Weiss, R. (1975): Loneliness. The Experience of Emotional and Social Isolation. Cambridge. MIT Press.

Westermarck, E. (1902): History of human marriage. Berlin. H. Barsdorf.

About the author

Dieter Adler is a qualified social worker and psychologist. He trained as a psychoanalyst with the German Psychoanalytic Association (DPV) and is a member of the DPV and the International Psychoanalytic Association (IPA). He has additional training in systemic family therapy, guided (or katathym) imaginative psychotherapy, child and adolescent psychotherapy, group analysis, and group psychotherapy as well as intensive psychodynamic short-term therapy (IS-TDP).

For thirty years he has been working in his own practice as a psychotherapist, psychoanalyst, group analyst, and child and adolescent psychotherapist with license to practice and health insurance approval.

He is a teaching therapist and supervisor in the training of psychotherapists. He has been supervising applications for psychotherapy from colleagues for twenty years. He is also an expert on psychotherapies provided by the health insurance funds and for therapies subsidized by the state.

He advises colleagues on setting up, managing, and optimizing their practices. Furthermore, he leads training events, workshops, symposia, and congresses. He is an expert for the Federal Association of Statutory Health Insurance Physicians and is the state aid in the guideline procedure.

He is involved in counseling for the gifted and highly gifted, writes books in this field, and is developing a test procedure to measure high sensitivity.

And, he is a filmmaker who has produced various documentaries and a (small) feature film. And a programmer and database developer on the side.

More books by Dieter Adler

Der Antrag auf psychodynamische Psychotherapie (The Application for psychodynamic psychotherapy). Giessen (3rd edition 2018). Psychosozial-Verlag.

Wie gründe und organisiere ich eine psychotherapeutische Praxis? (How do I Set up and Organize a Psychotherapeutic Practice?) Giessen (2020). Psychosozial-Verlag.

Gesundheitsdaten online - Telematik und elektronische Patientenakte - Chancen und Risiken von Datenmobilität und Datenaustausch (Health data Online - Telematics and Electronic Patient Files - Opportunities and Risks of Data Mobility and Data Exchange). Bonn (2018). Netzwerk-Verlag.

The Missing Manual - Das Handbuch der weniger bekannten und unbekannten psychotherapeutischen Interventionen (The Missing Manual - Handbook of the Lesser-Known and Unknown Psychotherapeutic Interventions. Bonn (2021). Netzwerk-Verlag.